Whales, Dolphins, and Porpoises of the World

Text and Illustrations
by Mary L. Baker

LEDAY & COMPANY · INC · GARDEN CITY · NEW YORK · 1987

ISBN 0-385-15366-X
Copyright © 1987 by Mary L. Baker
Printed in the United States of America
First Edition

Library of Congress Cataloging-in-Publication Data

Baker, M. L. (Mary L.)
  Whales, dolphins, and porpoises of the world.

  Bibliography: p. 220.
  1. Cetacea. I. Title.
QL737.C4B235 1987   599.5   86-2010

TO MY BELOVED FATHER AND MOTHER

Contents

Foreword

One of the things that has always held back the study of cetaceans (whales, dolphins, and porpoises) was the lack of good concepts of what their external appearance was. This is most evident in the lack, until just recently, of good illustrated guidebooks for the order. This is largely a problem of a dearth of research material, most cetaceans being known only from a few strandings.

Among other things, I am a student of cetacean natural history and taxonomy (the science of affixing names to various species). In reviewing the literature, I am amazed at the number of misidentifications of whales by apparently competent zoologists.

In January of 1973, six months after I had come to work for the Smithsonian Institution, I was faced with a rare species of whale that had stranded alive at Beach Haven, New Jersey. This was a member of the family Ziphiidae, the beaked whales, about which very little was known. Most of the names that had been applied to them were based on descriptions of adult males, in which two of the teeth form rather prominent tusks. The shapes of these tusks and their positions within the jaw differ between species. The only trouble is that these tusks erupt only in adult males. In females and juveniles the teeth do not erupt at all, and it turned out that this was a juvenile male. We delved through the literature on beaked whales and could come up with only the admonition, by a leading authority on beaked whale identification, that the only way to make a positive identification was to cut off the head, clean the skull, and take it around to a major museum and have it identified. This advice did not seem practical in this situation, because the whale was still alive and the local townspeople had become quite attached to it. We managed to put off the newspapers by telling them it was a beaked whale, but we were not sure which one, because there was not enough information to identify young males in the flesh. The animal eventually succumbed and we were able to X-ray the jaws to determine the shape and position of the teeth and identify it definitively as Blainville's beaked whale, *Mesoplodon densirostris.*

In retrospect, I have sympathy for any zoologist who is attempting to identify a whole whale or dolphin. With very few exceptions, there are a confusing array of related species to deal with. Whales and dolphins are variable animals, and where one species ends and another begins is sometimes difficult to ascertain.

Mary Baker is one of the few artists who can take photographs of a stranded whale and turn them into a good representation of what the live animal looked like. This book will do a great deal, not only in helping the reader to understand the amazing diversity of those animals that scientists term Cetacea, but also in giving them a better idea of what the animals may have looked like in their habitat.

JAMES G. MEAD
Smithsonian Institution

Preface

This book is an introduction to the lives of whales, dolphins, and porpoises and to the mysterious undersea world they inhabit. In order to serve as a guide, the text has been organized around a systematic classification of thirty-nine genera and seventy-five species, beginning with the small river dolphins and ending with the great right whales.

In the years required to research, write, and illustrate this survey, I have had the assistance of James G. Mead, Curator of Marine Mammals, Smithsonian Institution. Dr. Mead's advice on preparation, and the improvements made under his direction, have contributed in large measure to the successful development of the book.

Among the organizations and groups interested in this project, the support of my fellow trustees of the Oklahoma Zoological Society has been an indispensable help. At this time, I particularly want to express my appreciation to John and Eleanor Kirkpatrick, members of the Society, for their encouragement and support.

Of those who have been closely associated with my work, none have contributed more to its progress than Margaret and Henley Blair. It is with a sense of personal pleasure that I acknowledge a considerable debt to these friends for their loyalty and guidance. In areas requiring specialized knowledge, I am indebted to many other friends: to Senator David Boren and Anne Byrd for their help in solving problems; to Savoie Lottenville for his criticism and advice; to the late George M. Sutton for his very kind efforts in my behalf; and to Frances Nagle for her translations.

Among those who have actively shared in the preparatory work, I especially want to thank Florence Botchlet, who has brightened each day and typed the manuscript with an expert touch through many stages of development. I also would like to acknowledge the help provided by Shirley Mangan, of Information Management Consultants, who contacted centers of research worldwide to collect photographs and information on rare species.

I want to convey my appreciation to Doubleday & Company and to my editors and art director for the patience, courtesy and consideration shown at every point in the development of *Whales, Dolphins, and Porpoises of the World.*

MARY L. BAKER

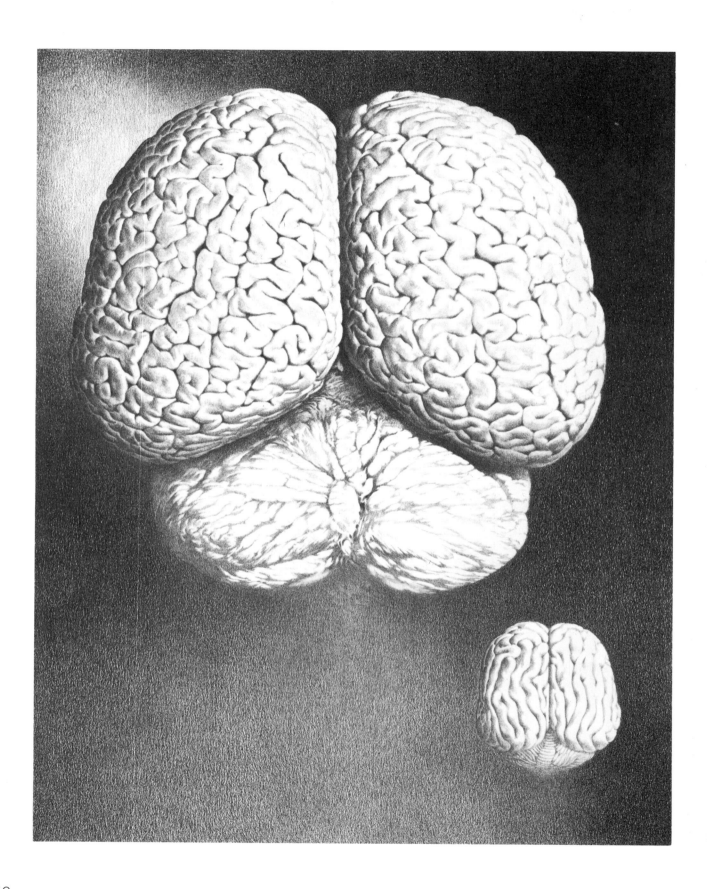

Anatomy of a Dolphin

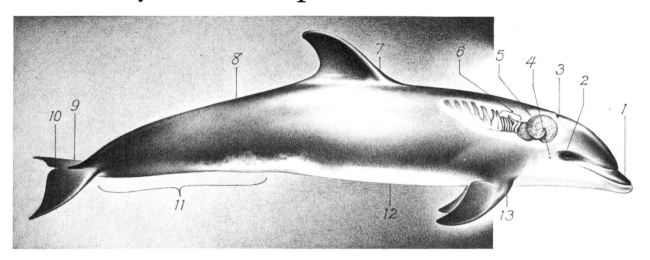

ABOVE: Outlines of dolphins with the locations of important anatomical features indicated. (1) rostrum, or beak, (2) eye, (3) blowhole, (4) auditory meatus, or ear, (5) brain, (6) cervical vertebrae, (7) dorsal fin, (8) dorsal surface (top), (9) flukes, (10) notch, (11) caudal section, (12) ventral surface, (13) flipper.

BELOW: Ventral surface of male and female dolphins. (1) male, (2) navel, (3) genital slit, (4) anus, (5) two mammary slits, (6) female.

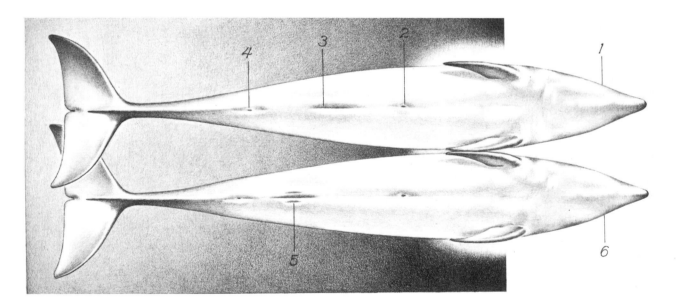

OPPOSITE PAGE: The large brain of a fin whale compared to the small brain of a blind susu (fin-whale brain, top left, after a photograph by Ries and Langworthy; susu brain, lower right, after Anderson).

River dolphins: from top, susu, boutu, baiji, and franciscana. (Please note that some illustrations of the whales, dolphins, and porpoises are not strictly proportional.)

River Dolphins, Platanistidae

All whales, dolphins, and porpoises belong to Cetacea, a major order of completely aquatic mammals that contains two groups, or suborders, of living whales: the toothed whales, Odontoceti, and the baleen (or whalebone) whales, Mysticeti. This survey opens with the list of toothed whales, introduced by the platanistids, a very special family of dolphins.

The little river dolphins are primitive in form, showing far less specialization in body structure when compared with true dolphins of the family Delphinidae. For this reason, they have been placed in a separate family, called the Platanistidae. Among the primitive characteristics retained by the dolphins are eight pairs of double-headed ribs; cervical vertebrae that are not fused (a feature common among primitive cetaceans); a relatively symmetrical skull; and a very long, slender beak lined with an array of needlelike teeth numbering from 100 up to a maximum of 242.

The dolphins are small, with broad paddle-like flippers and a low dorsal fin or ridge. Gentle and inquisitive, they pass their entire lives in the waters of large rivers and estuaries in South America and Asia. Listed below are the river dolphins, with their common names, classifications, and numbers of species. On the following pages are descriptions of the four dolphins.

GANGES SUSU
  OTHER COMMON NAMES: Ganges River dolphin, gangetic dolphin, blind dolphin
  GENUS: *Platanista*
  SPECIES: Ganges susu, *Platanista gangetica,* the single recognized species
    Indus susu, *Platanista minor (= indi),* is usually regarded as being synonymous with *Platanista gangetica*

BOUTU
  OTHER COMMON NAMES: Amazon dolphin, bouto, boto, bufeo, pink porpoise
  GENUS: *Inia*
  SPECIES: boutu, *Inia geoffrensis,* the single species

BAIJI
  OTHER COMMON NAMES: ji (200 B.C.), white dolphin, Chinese dolphin, white flag dolphin
  GENUS: *Lipotes*
  SPECIES: baiji, *Lipotes vexillifer,* the single species

FRANCISCANA
  OTHER COMMON NAME: La Plata River dolphin
  GENUS: *Pontoporia*
  SPECIES: franciscana, *Pontoporia blainvillei,* the single species

Susu and young in river channel.

Ganges Susu

Platanista gangetica

In the hour before dusk, when late sunlight floods the broad surface of the Ganges River with crimson and gold, the dark gray forms of a small dolphin and her calf drift out of deeper shadows toward the light. As they move forward, the clicking sonar, or sound probe, of the mother dolphin outlines the shape of the riverbed and a mass of twisted roots nearby. Far downriver, it identifies a long-nosed Indian crocodile striding across the main channel. Returning echoes of the invisible sound waves even transmit the shape and texture of a skull resting among rounded stones on the riverbed.

To feel her way, the susu, or Ganges dolphin, *Platanista gangetica,* sends out a series of high-pitched clicks. These intensely sharp sounds race through the water, sometimes traveling rapidly over a great distance to strike objects and return to the dolphin, entering through the bone structure of the lower jaw and skull to reach her extremely sensitive inner ears. Such vibrating sound waves, or sonar, appear to identify objects not only by form, but also by density and texture. The small dolphin listens to these vibrations with all her body, even her bones; for the susu is blind, unable to see the twisted roots, the ambling crocodile, or the young dolphin that touches her side for reassurance because it, too, is blind and has been so since birth.

Giorgio Pilleri, in an excellent study of the susu, *Die Geheimnisse der blinden Delphine,* theorizes that the blindness of these dolphins may have developed after they were cut off from clear coastal waters and the bordering sea millions of years ago and were forced to adapt to the murky waters of the Ganges, Brahmaputra, and Indus rivers of India and Pakistan. In this silt-filled environment, the structure of their eyes deteriorated: the lens atrophied and vanished, the iris lost its function, and the heavy optic nerve eventually was reduced to a mere thread, with the ganglion of light-trans-

Blind dolphin using flipper touch for guidance.

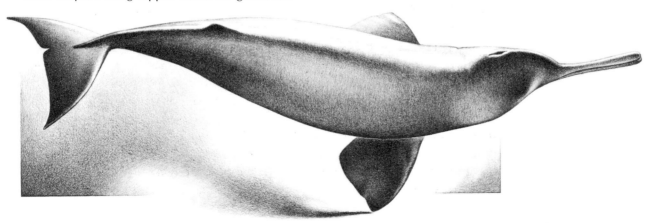

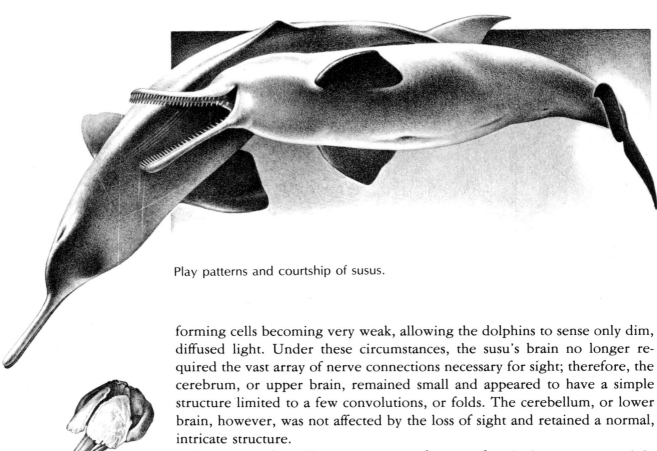

Play patterns and courtship of susus.

Skull of susu
with shell-like
maxillary crests.

forming cells becoming very weak, allowing the dolphins to sense only dim, diffused light. Under these circumstances, the susu's brain no longer required the vast array of nerve connections necessary for sight; therefore, the cerebrum, or upper brain, remained small and appeared to have a simple structure limited to a few convolutions, or folds. The cerebellum, or lower brain, however, was not affected by the loss of sight and retained a normal, intricate structure.

Compact and small, susus measure 6 to 7.9 feet (1.8 to 2.4 meters) in overall length. Females are slightly larger than males and have a longer beak but appear to be less active and aggressive. Color is limited to dark grayish brown or lead black on the back, fading to a paler shade below. The flippers are broad and appear to be almost square, spreading out in a fanlike shape. Instead of a dorsal fin, a well-defined ridge rises to a low peak near the center of the back, then continues as a raised edge down the upper caudal area to flukes that are wide and have a center notch.

Apart from its eyes and brain, the head of a susu has been altered in other ways. Its blowhole is a slitlike orifice opening longitudinally on top of its head, instead of across the head as in other dolphins. Internally, the two small frontal bones found in the skulls of most dolphins are replaced, in susus, by two massive bony plates called the maxillary crests, which project upward and forward in a shell-like structure from either side of the skull, then curve inward to almost touch near the nasal area, an arrangement that may function as a baffle to control incoming sounds and also direct and intensify outgoing sounds.

In order to bring the full range of its highly refined sonar system into focus with the aid of the great maxillary crests, the dolphin swims on its side with its near-blind eyes sensing the pale light of the moon spread in a silver stain on the dark water above. On its lower side, a large flipper, lined on the outer edge with rows of sensitive nerves, is extended to touch the riverbed for guidance in turning; thus oriented, the dolphin moves its head up and down to sweep the river with its powerful sonar from a side position.

Susus become active in late afternoon, when shadows grow long and the sun moves low on the horizon. They gather in small groups to search for food, each one locating a school of fish, then pursuing a single fish vigorously until the quarry is captured, thoroughly bitten, and swallowed head first. Their long, slender beaks can open to a 90° angle, and the 29 to 37 needlelike teeth that line each side of the upper and lower jaws interlock to present an almost solid band of gleaming ivory.

A significant discovery concerned the incessant motion of the dolphin hour after hour, day after day, when its swimming movements appeared to proceed without rest in what may have been a conditioned reflex to the river's powerful current. Since motion was continuous, the question of sleep and a renewal of energy required an answer.

The first indication of rest became evident when a pause of one to seven seconds, occurring at regular intervals, was detected in the clicking sounds of the dolphin. During these intervals, it drifted forward with slight movement. This pattern of rest is called polyphasic, a kind of micro sleep. Tested over a period of time, it was found that these short, continuous naps were adding up, within a span of twenty-four hours, to a normal period of sleep.

By easy stages, susus wander in a local migration along familiar waterways. When winter settles in, they leave the sluggish streams to find shelter in the depths of major rivers flowing low in their beds during the dry season with only the broad main channel remaining deep enough to protect the dolphins. Covered by these warm waters, they wait until the heavy rains of spring begin to fill the watercourse with a rising tide. Liberated by fresh, swift currents, the dolphins swim past rice fields and scattered villages until they finally reach the quiet streams and deep woodland pools of remote areas.

Little blind dolphins in summer.

There the little blind susus gather to mate and bear their young. In quiet nooks, many of the females give birth to grayish-white calves measuring 27 to 29 inches (68 to 73 centimeters) in length and weighing 15 pounds (7 kilograms). Scattered among the connecting waterways, other dolphins separate into small groups or pairs to begin the ancient ritual of courtship.

At times the water swirls with fast-moving susus caught up in the excitement of high emotion when a male chases an eligible female at top speed, biting at her back or side with a force that leaves the marks of his sharp teeth on her skin. In a solicitous mood, the male will press his side against the motionless female, or stroke her, in passing, with his flipper. Affection is expressed in a gentle way when one nibbles at the fin of another, or two dolphins nestle close together, to the accompaniment of soft, chirping notes.

Range of susu.

Boutus hunting in the clouded waters of the Amazon River.

Boutu

Inia geoffrensis

The Amazon River flows across the continent of South America from the towering slopes of the Andes Mountains in the west to the Atlantic Coast in the east, traversing one of the most magnificent rain forests on earth, a strange and lavishly beautiful hylaea, which forms the great drainage basin of the Amazon in Brazil. It is in this vast scenic land, in the rolling brown waters of the river, that the boutu, or Amazon dolphin, *Inia geoffrensis,* makes its home.

The boutu attains a length of 6 to 9.75 feet (1.8 to 3 meters), and a weight of 200 to 275 pounds (90 to 125 kilograms). Its beak is long and slender, turning slightly downward near the tip. The top of its head is distinctly rounded, and the eyes are small, set above broadly curved cheeks which obstruct lower vision to such a degree that the dolphin must turn on its side or upside down to examine objects on the river floor. In place of a dorsal fin, there is a low ridge which extends along the mid-back to the base of the flukes. Flippers are very broad and flexible, and the wide flukes, spread in a half circle, are unusually large.

Color is variable among these dolphins. Recent reports suggest that their light skin may turn darker in shallow water when exposed to strong sunlight over a long period of time. Young individuals are gray or blackish above, changing to a medium gray below. Adults are blue-gray, becoming lighter with age, then fading to a pale gray, pinkish, or even a delicate rosy cream color.

In the tropical winter, when heavy rains cause the Amazon River to rise 30 to 39 feet (9 to 12 meters) and overflow vast areas of the forest, venturesome dolphins travel far afield. They leave the main channel to explore the high water of flooded lowlands that stretches as far as the eye can see, pierced by massive tree trunks and trailing liana vines. Boutus appear to lack the instinctive caution of other river dwellers, wandering far from the safety of deep river channels and familiar territory into areas of potential danger from receding floodwaters or the attacks of large predators. Young boutus display this lack of fear by sleeping on their backs or sides, in a complete reversal of the usual dorsal-side-up position.

Swimming alone or in pairs, at times gathering in random groups of up to six individuals, they glide close to the bottom, threading through the swaying stems of tall river plants or strands of algae on the branches of sunken trees. Within its tapered beak, each dolphin is equipped with a formidable array of 24 to 34 slender, sharply pointed teeth lining each side of the upper and lower jaws. Even piranhas, savage little fish that are feared for their butchery, fall easy prey to a boutu's small but efficient teeth. Probing with their long beaks, they test the algae for hidden snails or pry beneath matted

Young boutus sleeping on their backs in a rare reversal of the normal position (Caldwell).

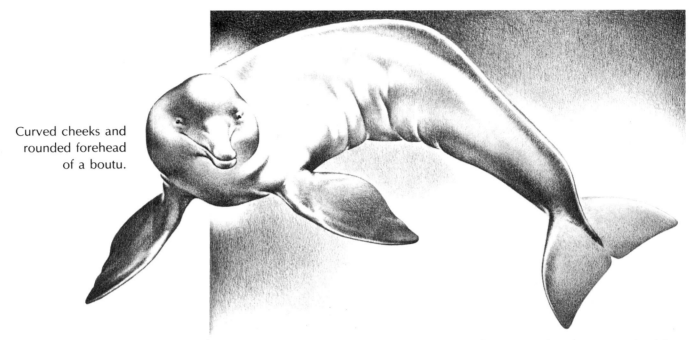

Curved cheeks and rounded forehead of a boutu.

Piranhas in the Amazon River.

leaves to uncover any lurking crabs or small prawns, leaving a swirl of fine sediment to drift in the turbid current.

Vision is probably good, but the senses of hearing and touch are more highly developed and more useful in rolling floodwaters and the film of silt that often fills the river with a brown, opaque cloudiness. Using echolocation to scan these murky waters, the dolphins sweep the tangled debris and channeled floor in search of mud-dwelling turtles, crustaceans, and mollusks that wander on the river bottom. A report of food items listed snails, crabs, prawns, turtles, catfish, and a variety of other freshwater fish.

Among Amazon dolphins, birth occurs from July through September. The newborn infant is darker in color, measuring around 30 inches (76 centimeters), with a soft, rubbery skin that creases into vertical folds on its small, flexible body. Amiable and affectionate by nature, there is evidence of a continuing attachment among the members of a family, because young dolphins may remain with their mothers until they are almost adult size.

Their lives are passed in the deep channels of the Amazon River from the juncture of the Tocantins River in the east, 1,550 miles (2,500 kilometers) across the continent of South America to Nauta and Iquitos, Peru, with large numbers reported traveling upriver, at times accompanied by groups of tucuxi, or little bay dolphins. Amazon dolphins are known to pass from the Amazon River into the northern Orinoco River through a connection with the Casiquiare River, flowing near the border of Venezuela.

Boutus are freshwater dolphins, confined to inland waterways and therefore vulnerable. In coming decades, when the immense territory of the Amazon Basin is opened up to industry and settlement, the river will be filled with the heavy traffic of barges carrying oil, fertilizers, chemical products, and other contaminants. When development reaches this point, these quaint, gentle dolphins will suffer severe hardship and a population decline that may reach extinction.

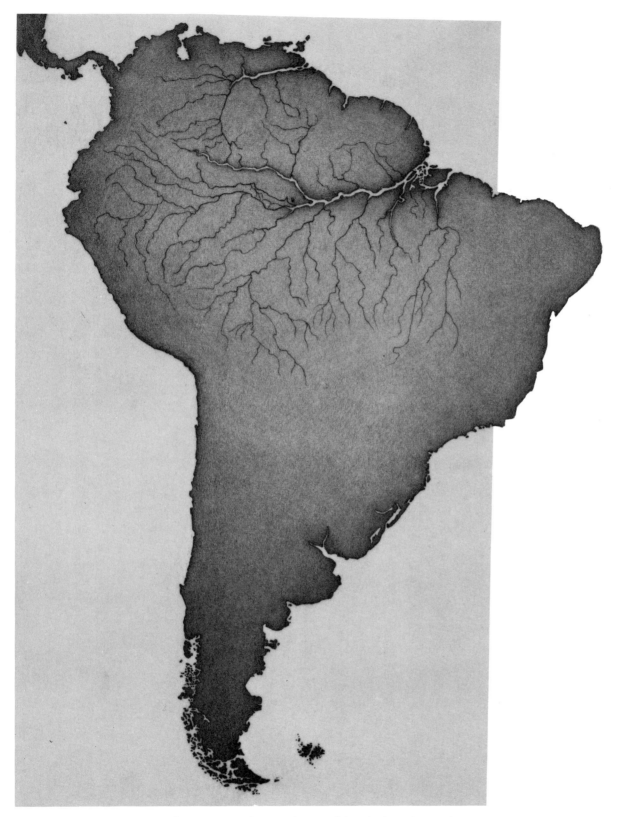

The mighty Amazon River flows across the continent of South America and
connects with the northern Orinoco River.

Baiji in the shallow waters of Changjiang (or Yangtze River).

Baiji

Lipotes vexillifer

Long ago in ancient China, a legend was told of the tragic death of a beautiful princess who threw herself into the dark waters of Dongting (Tung Ting) Lake and drowned. It was said that her spirit assumed the form of a small, pale dolphin and lived forever after in the depths of the placid lake. In this way, the Chinese people have explained down through the centuries the presence of a little dolphin in a great freshwater lake in the center of their fabled land.

Known by the ancient name of *ji* or *baiji,* the Chinese dolphin, *Lipotes vexillifer,* has a recorded history spanning more than two thousand years. The oldest surviving record was found to have been written in the time of the West Han Dynasty in the book Erh-ya (200 B.C.), which makes the terse statement "Ji is a dolphin," later elaborated by Kuo-p'u (A.D. 276–324) in a more extensive and detailed description. Other accounts were produced in the eleventh, eighteenth, and nineteenth centuries. Then, in 1923, an article titled "The White-Flag Dolphin of the Tung Ting Lake" was published by C. M. Hoy, followed by a similar article in 1940 by C. H. Pope. Thereafter, for several decades, no news came out of China.

Recently, a fourteen-page document containing the history, description, present condition, and distribution of this mysterious dolphin was delivered to the Smithsonian Institution. It was written by Zhou Kaiya, Ch'ian Weichuan, and Li Yuemin and was titled "Investigations on the Distribution of the Baiji *(Lipotes vexillifer* Miller)."

The following account is based on the information contained in this document.

Plump and moderately small, the baiji attains a length ranging from 4.6 to 8.2 feet (1.4 to 2.5 meters), with females usually larger than males. Girth measures up to a hefty 5.5 feet (1.7 meters), and weight varies widely, depending on individual health, with one long but lean dolphin 6.5 feet (2 meters) in length weighing 121 pounds (55 kilograms), while a second specimen, five feet (1.5 meters) long, weighed 159 pounds (72 kilograms). Maximum weight is listed at approximately 522 pounds (237 kilograms).

The dolphin's head is spherical and shows a steep upward curve from beak to forehead, ending in a small crease, or dimple, in back of the head. Its eyes are placed above the corner of the mouth, and its blowhole, rounded and rather long, is situated more to the left side of the head. The auditory meatus, or ear canal, is a tiny hole opening below and behind the eye. The long, narrow beak shows a slight upward curve at the tip and a projecting lower jaw. Lining each side of the upper and lower jaws are 30 to 35 small teeth covered with a layer of enamel roughened on top by serrated ridges, similar to the teeth of the rough-toothed dolphin.

The dorsal fin, broad-based and triangular, is situated past the middle of

Two young dolphins exploring the river's depths.

Baiji: lateral, ventral, and dorsal views.

the back, flippers are wide with a rounded tip, and the spread of the flukes equals one fourth of the dolphin's length. From dorsal fin to flukes, the body narrows dramatically, tapering from a robust midsection to a small tail stock. All of the upper body, including the back, dorsal fin, flippers, and flukes, is slate blue-gray, dark on the upper beak, forehead, and head, then changing to pale blue-gray on the sides and on a small area in front of the flippers. The lower edges of the beak, the sides of the head and lower surface of the body are pale gray or a gleaming ivory white.

Covered by the deep waters of the Changjiang (or Yangtze River), surrounded by its rolling current, the dolphins gather in groups of five to ten to hunt for food along overhanging banks or the furrowed riverbed. Their slender beaks are adept at searching through the soft mud covering the bottom of the river, probing among the tall stems of reeds, prying through a tangled web of roots to dislodge the long, eel-like catfish and delicate freshwater shrimp they are fond of. Drifting through the broad waterways and lingering near sandbars, they are sometimes joined by groups of Chinese finless porpoises, the small dark-gray porpoises that have wandered through the great rivers of China throughout history. The contrast in color between a pale baiji (white dolphin) and the dark porpoise is striking.

Although little information has been obtained on the breeding and birth of these dolphins, examination of stranded specimens has indicated that the birth of their young probably occurs around May. Baiji usually have one calf, but twins are not rare. In newborn dolphins, the teeth are not developed and the beak is short, with little whiskers appearing at the corners of the mouth.

Distribution of this small Chinese dolphin is far more widespread than had been realized. Once thought to be confined to Dongting Lake, baiji are now known to prefer the great Changjiang system. In past decades, as the surface of Dongting Lake slowly sank and mud patches became more numerous, the dolphins were forced to abandon its shrinking cover for the more comfortable depths of Poyang Lake, in Jiangxi Province, where they assembled in large numbers, particularly around the deep entrance of the lake.

Local migrations occur during the summer, but by late fall, most of the dolphins have returned to the Changjiang. As winter's cold touches the grain stubble in the fields with white frost and topples cattails along the bank, the broad surface of the river begins to recede, its level sinking until gently sloping banks turn into broad mud flats, and only in the wide main channel does the water level remain high above groups of dolphins scattered along its length. Confined to more restricted quarters but sheltered by the warm river water, they pass the cold, stormy months of winter in relative comfort, waiting for bright sunlight and the fresh rains of spring to flood the river, releasing them once more to wander through the provinces of Hubei, Anhwi, northern Hunan, Jiangxi, Zhejiang and Jiangsu, wherever the rolling brown waters of the great Changjiang flow.

The ancient Changjiang, home of the baiji, flows across central China.

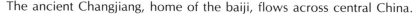
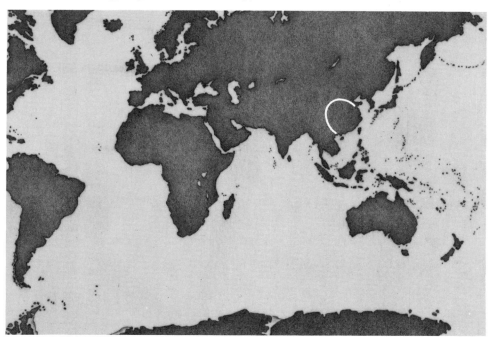

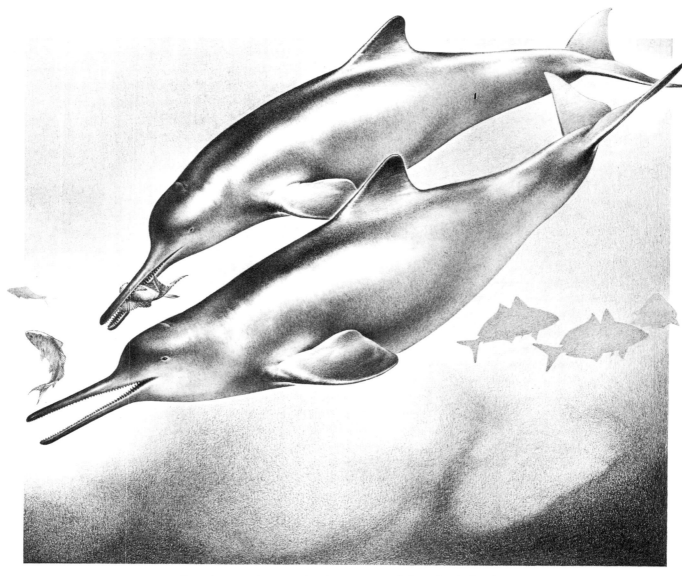

Franciscanas foraging in the estuary of the Río de la Plata.

Franciscana
Pontoporia blainvillei

The franciscana, *Pontoporia blainvillei,* is the smallest member of the four dolphins listed in the ancient family of Platanistidae, or river dolphins, measuring approximately 5 to 5.5 feet (1.5 to 1.75 meters) when fully grown and weighing from 64 to 135 pounds (29 to 61 kilograms). Among the living members of this family, which include the Ganges susu, the boutu, and the baiji (all river dwellers), only the franciscana is known to prefer the waters of estuaries and coastal areas open to the sea.

Pontoporia is highly specialized, both internally and externally. Its beak is remarkably long and slender, with 50 to 60 sharply pointed, needlelike teeth lining each side of the upper and lower jaws. According to records, the overall extension of its beak, relative to body length, is longer than that of any other cetacean. Its seven cervical vertebrae also are unusual. Instead of being fused together like those of true dolphins, the vertebrae in its neck (as in the other three river dolphins) are entirely separate, allowing more flexible movement of the head and neck in bending or turning. The dorsal fin, midway on its back, is triangular, with a distinct ridge continuing down the back to the flukes; flippers are broad, with a semiround outline, while flukes are pointed and have a well-defined median notch.

Cusk eel.

Conger eel.

Most of these dolphins are pale brown or a darker brownish gray above and a lighter shade below. On some individuals, the sides and upper surface of the body are stained with a sulphur-yellow film caused by diatoms (tiny, one-celled plants that flourish in sunlit waters). Swimming through floating rafts of these minute plants, the dolphins acquire a temporary coloring similar to the yellow tint on the underside of a great blue whale.

Sleek and graceful, franciscanas gather in small family groups, skimming close over sun-dappled sand in shallow zones to probe the uneven layers of shelving banks, where decades of erosion have dislodged loose rubble from the broken strata, leaving deep holes or dark, concealing crevices. In these crumbling walls, small conger eels find homes by pressing their long gray bodies into convenient cracks, venturing out only to stalk a passing octopus or crab, and becoming, in turn, food for the franciscanas.

In rocks piled below the walls, the dolphins hunt for slender cusk eels, then drift down through the green depths to find cutlass fish, a favorite food item in summer, or probe dark hollows on the ocean floor searching for midshipman fish, a pugnacious member of the toadfish family known for its large mouth and quick temper. In deeper waters, rough scad and glittering shoals of silvery anchovy or mullet are closely followed by the hungry dolphins. Armed with 242 needlelike teeth, the long, slender beak of *Pontoporia*

Mother dolphin and young.

is superbly equipped to seize and hold soft-bodied eels, scaled fish, or the boneless forms of squid and octopus that hide among the rocks and seaweed.

When winter comes to the southern hemisphere, many of the dolphins leave the coastal waters of the Río de la Plata, where they had remained through the months of summer, and are thought to wander out to sea or journey northward along the coast of Brazil toward a warmer climate. They are the only members of the family of river dolphins that customarily enter oceanic waters and risk the dangers of the open sea.

Franciscanas that stray too far may fall prey to roving killer whales, or they may be attacked by sharks, perhaps by a seven-gill shark that sometimes leaves the deeper and darker regions of the ocean to prowl along the coast of Uruguay and Argentina. Coming up from black depths around 1,300 feet (400 meters), the shark moves at a languid pace, its movements quickening as it draws near land to cruise silently between the scattered colonies of sea lions in search of young pups or careless adults. The small size of franciscanas, their neutral color of medium or dark gray, which blends into the haziness of the water, and their quiet habits may afford some protection by making them less conspicuous than larger dolphins or noisy seals and sea lions.

The birth of infant dolphins is believed to occur sometime between October and January. These newborn young are incredibly small, measuring only 27 inches (70 centimeters) in length. A report from Robert Brownell, Jr., of the Smithsonian stated that two unborn young collected from Uruguayan waters in 1975 had a body length equal to 44.5 percent of the mother's length. Their beaks were very short and their color was a soft brownish white, often marked by a darker band along the midback.

Limited to the coastal waters of the Atlantic along the eastern shores of South America, the present range of franciscanas centers in the estuary of the Río de la Plata (the River Plate) and extends from Ubatuba, Brazil, near the Tropic of Capricorn, south to the Valdés Peninsula, in Argentina. Although the dolphins are well established in the Río de la Plata estuary, there is no record of a franciscana entering the Uruguay or the Paraná rivers, which are tributaries of the estuary.

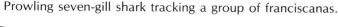
Prowling seven-gill shark tracking a group of franciscanas.

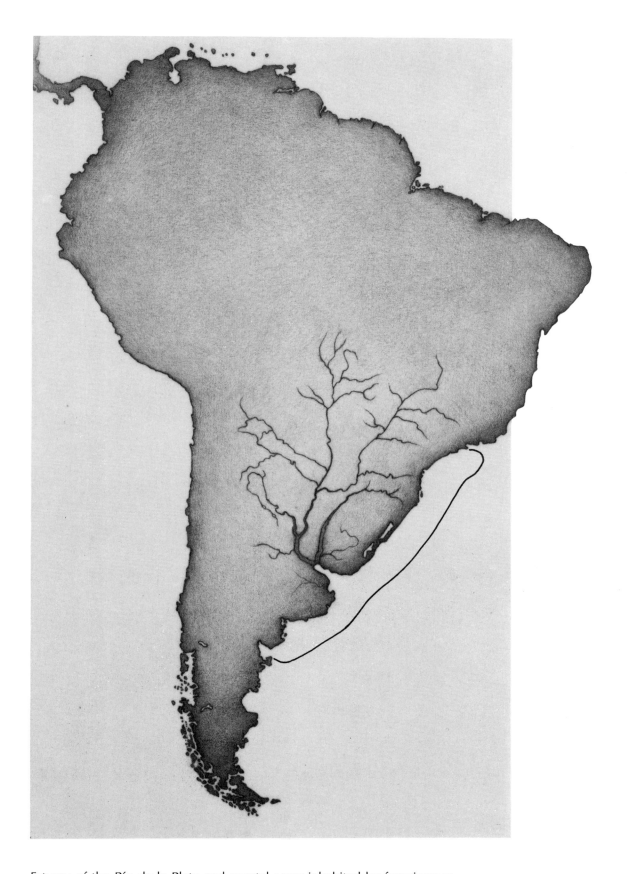

Estuary of the Río de la Plata and coastal areas inhabited by franciscanas.

Beaked whales: True's beaked whale (above) and Cuvier's beaked whale (below).

Beaked Whales, Ziphiidae

The rarest and most mysterious of all living cetaceans are the beaked whales of the family Ziphiidae, a group which contains five genera and approximately eighteen species. Like the river dolphins, they have certain characteristics which serve as an identification guide. These include one or two pairs of large functional teeth situated at the tip, center, or back of the lower jaw; a definite beak; two to six short throat grooves; and a dorsal fin placed well past the midpoint of the back. Flippers are small, and the broad flukes have no notch.

The beaked whales are usually rotund, with a rather small head and a fusiform, or spindle-shaped, body. Some of the species produce spermaceti, like the great sperm whale, and most of them have scars in the form of pale spots or long, linear streaks. While males habitually fight among themselves and are often heavily scarred, there is growing evidence that females and young also are attacked in certain seasons.

Since these whales are seldom observed, detailed records are kept of each identified specimen. Anyone who finds a rare whale, dolphin, or porpoise should notify the nearest regional office of the National Marine Fisheries Service.

Listed below are two of the beaked whales, with their common names, classifications, and the numbers of species in their genera. The remaining three genera follow in a separate section.

TRUE'S BEAKED WHALE
 OTHER COMMON NAME: none
 GENUS: *Mesoplodon*
 SPECIES: The genus *Mesoplodon* includes twelve species at this time:
  True's beaked whale, *Mesoplodon mirus*
  Longman's beaked whale, *Mesoplodon pacificus*
  Sowerby's beaked whale, *Mesoplodon bidens*
  Blainville's beaked whale, *Mesoplodon densirostris*
  Gervais' beaked whale, *Mesoplodon europaeus*
  Strap-toothed whale, *Mesoplodon layardii*
  Gray's beaked whale, *Mesoplodon grayi*
  Hector's beaked whale, *Mesoplodon hectori*
  Stejneger's beaked whale, *Mesoplodon stejnegeri*
  Andrews' beaked whale, *Mesoplodon bowdoini*
  Ginkgo-toothed beaked whale, *Mesoplodon ginkgodens*
  Hubbs' beaked whale, *Mesoplodon carlhubbsi*

CUVIER'S BEAKED WHALE
 OTHER COMMON NAMES: Cuvier's whale, goose-beaked whale, two-toothed whale
 GENUS: *Ziphius*
 SPECIES: Cuvier's beaked whale, *Ziphius cavirostris,* the single species

Dorsal, lateral, and ventral views of True's beaked whale, *M. mirus.*

True's Beaked Whale
Mesoplodon mirus

The twelve species of whales that form the genus *Mesoplodon* are noted for certain unique features of the skull, jaws, and teeth, especially the rodlike bones forming the rostrum, or beak. These bones owe their unusual density to a gradual hardening of cartilage which eventually combines with the bone material in the upper jaw. In *M. densirostris,* a species of *Mesoplodon,* this process forms a mass of compacted bone so dense that the specific gravity of the whale's rostrum is $33^{1/3}$ percent greater than that of elephant ivory.

True's beaked whale, *Mesoplodon mirus,* is typical of the genus. Its length ranges from 16 to 17.5 feet (4.9 to 5.3 meters). The head is small, with a well-defined beak, a rounded forehead, and a slight depression around the blowhole. Its body is robust in midsection, tapering down to a slender tail stock with a clearly defined ridge extending to wide flukes. The dorsal fin is falcate (sickle-shaped), rising well past the midpoint of the back; flippers are small and placed rather high on the sides, while the flukes occasionally may have a very slight indication of a center notch. The throat is marked by two grooves converging in a V shape.

Both male and female whales of *M. mirus* usually have two teeth embedded in the gums of the lower jaw. These teeth are not visible in females, but all adult males develop one or two pairs of large teeth in the lower jaw which are compressed laterally, set obliquely in their sockets, and may be visible above the gum line, a characteristic shared by Cuvier's beaked whales and northern bottlenose whales.

The number, position, and structure of teeth are very important in identifying toothed whales. All species of *Mesoplodon* have a pair of teeth which are always situated in the lower jaw. Since the position and structure of these teeth provide an important guide in separating the twelve species, their location is usually listed, along with the whale's size, shape, and color. In some species, the teeth are found at the tip of the mandible, or lower jaw, while in others they appear far back at the angle of the gape, or corner of the mouth, and a few are situated at the mandibular symphysis, or the back edge of the place where the two sides of the lower jaw are joined.

True's beaked whales are dark gray or dull black on the back and lighter on the side, overlaid by a fine spotting of black, then fading to pale gray or dull white below. A dark gray line may mark the center of the abdomen, and a small irregular white patch appears on the genital area. Both sides of the

The lower jaw of *M. bidens,* a species of *Mesoplodon,* showing the point of mandibular symphysis, where the two sides of the lower jaw are joined; a tooth; and position of the tooth at the mandibular symphysis (Van Beneden and Gervais).

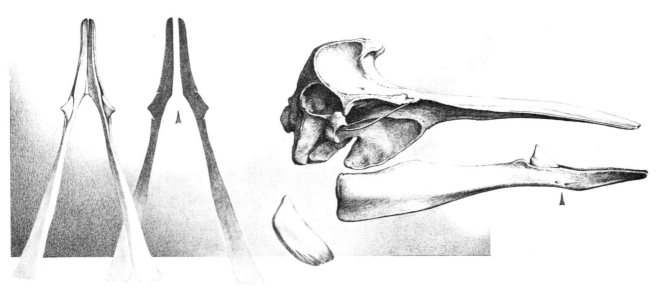

Female and young
of *M. mirus.*

flippers and flukes are dark. Random spots, or larger splotches of pale gray, are scattered over the dark gray back and sides, interspersed by parallel white streaks, probably the raking cut of a rival male's teeth, which crisscross the back with scars.

In temperate waters off the Middle Atlantic States of the U.S.A., the coast spreads out below the surface of the ocean in a great sunken plateau called the continental shelf. From shallow coastal waters, this vast, submerged table-land descends gradually to deeper water at the edge of the shelf, then plunges down the steep, furrowed continental slope into the blackness of abyssal depths. Groups of True's beaked whales pass over this continental slope to dive deep in search of wandering schools of squid and small fish. Seldom seen and virtually unknown, *M. mirus* has been sighted in the North Atlantic, particularly in an area bounded by Cape Breton Island, Nova Scotia, in the north, and Flagler Beach, Florida, in the south. It is also known from Ireland (three records) and South Africa (seven records).

The pairing of these rare whales takes place in late winter and early spring. After a period of twelve months, the females give birth to calves measuring around 6.8 feet (2.1 meters), about 40 percent of adult length.

Of the many species that make up the genus *Mesoplodon,* most are relatively unknown and several could be considered aberrant. Poorly defined and based on inadequate information, these numerous types may eventually be reduced, after thorough study, to a few well-documented members. The following twelve species are listed under *Mesoplodon.*

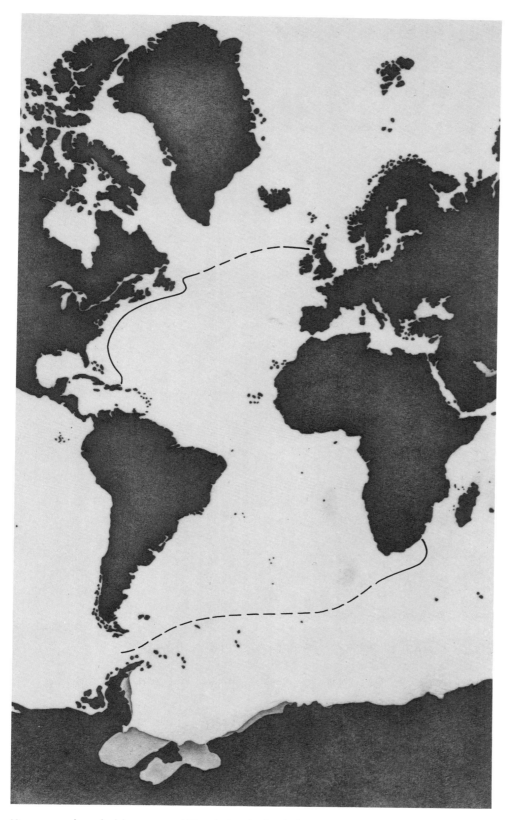

Known and probable range of True's beaked whale.

SPECIES OF *MESOPLODON*

Longman's Beaked Whale, *Mesoplodon pacificus.* Little is known about this relatively large whale. All present information is based on a skull over 3.3 feet (1 meter) in length, found in Australia in 1926, and a second skull discovered in 1955 in Somalia, Africa.

Sowerby's Beaked Whale, *Mesoplodon bidens* **(A).** *M. bidens* is around 16 feet (5 meters) long with a slender head, a high, slightly falcate dorsal fin, and unnotched tail flukes that have a partially concave rear border. Its dark gray or bluish-black body, sometimes showing gray or white on the underside, is marked by multiple white scars. The jaws are often edged with white, and each side of the lower jaw has a tooth midway between the tip of the beak and the corner of the mouth. Sowerby's whale is found only in the far North Atlantic Ocean.

Blainville's Beaked Whale, *Mesoplodon densirostris* **(B).** In this rare whale, the development of two teeth in the lower jaw of a male reaches massive proportions, with subsequent enlargement of the surrounding bones into wedge-shaped prominences containing two great teeth that are barely exposed and placed near the angle of the gape (or corner of the mouth). The whale's length is around 17 feet (5.2 meters). Its body is spindle-shaped, with small, pointed flippers and a triangular or falcate dorsal fin situated far down the back. Color is dark gray or black above, fading to a lighter gray below, with irregular grayish-white spots. *M. densirostris* is found worldwide in temperate and tropical seas.

Gervais' Beaked Whale, *Mesoplodon europaeus* **(C).** This whale is slender, with a very small head and a narrow beak containing a pair of teeth placed in the lower jaw at the juncture of the mandible. Length is 22 feet (6.7 meters). The dorsal fin is triangular or falcate, flippers are low on the sides, and flukes are unnotched. In *M. europaeus,* the back is grayish black, and the abdomen a lighter gray. Rarely seen, these whales are found in the western Atlantic from Long Island to the West Indies, with one stranded whale recorded from the English Channel.

Strap-toothed Whale, *Mesoplodon layardii* **(D).** The two teeth of *M. layardii* are greatly modified and show a radical departure in their growth pattern. Instead of being conical, they are long, flat-sided, and sharp. In male whales, these two tusks continue to grow outward and upward, curving over to form a single straplike arch above the upper jaw in a manner that may eventually impede its movements.

Considered to be the largest member of *Mesoplodon,* the strap-toothed whale reaches a length of around 16 to 20 feet (5 to 6 meters). The beak, throat, and ventral area of adult whales are white, the forehead and forepart of the back are brownish gray, and the rest of the body is brownish black with numerous scars. Immature whales are dark gray on top and lighter below. *M. layardii* is found near Australia, New Zealand, South Africa, Uruguay, and the Falkland Islands.

Species of *Mesoplodon:* from top, Sowerby's beaked whale, *M. bidens;* Blainville's beaked whale, *M. densirostris;* Gervais' beaked whale, *M. europaeus;* strap-toothed whale, *M. layardii* (after a drawing by G. J. B. Ross).

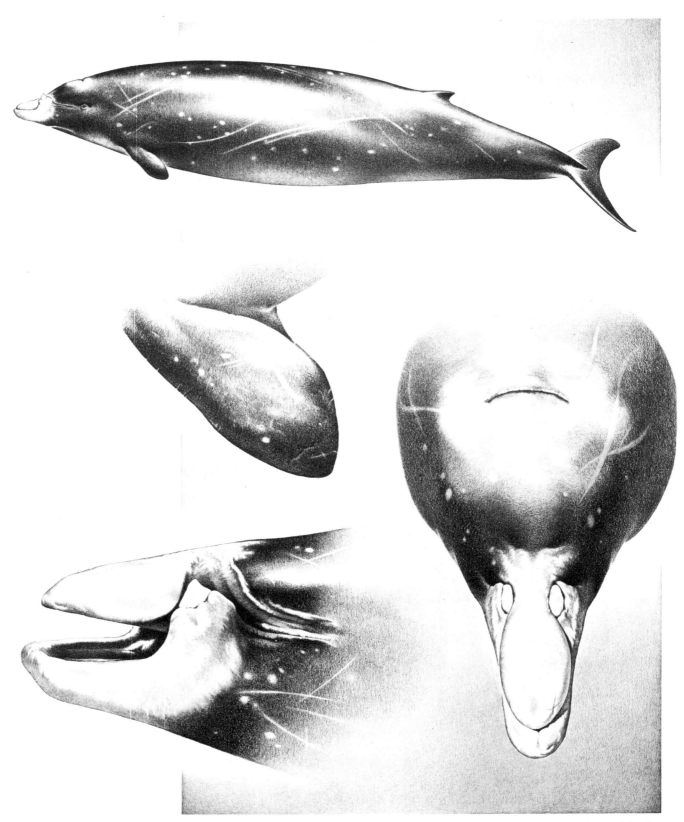

Hubbs' beaked whale, *M. carlhubbsi,* a species of *Mesoplodon.* Outline of body form, flipper, open mouth, and top of head (showing blowhole and teeth on either side of the constricted upper beak).

Dorsal, ventral, and lateral views of Gray's beaked whale (above). Lateral view of Hector's beaked whale (below).

Gray's Beaked Whale, *Mesoplodon grayi* **(A, B, C).** Often called the southern beaked whale or scamperdown whale, Gray's beaked whale has a pair of small teeth at the mandibular symphysis of the lower jaw. Length extends to 20 feet (6 meters) and color is varied, with dark gray-green above, changing to brownish gray or white below. Range includes Australia, New Zealand, South America, South Africa, and the Netherlands.

Hector's Beaked Whale, *Mesoplodon hectori* **(D).** This very rare whale has two flat, triangular teeth at the tip of the lower jaw. Length to 14.5 feet (4.4 meters). It has been recorded in the southern hemisphere and near California.

SPECIES OF *MESOPLODON*

Stejneger's Beaked Whale, *Mesoplodon stejnegeri* **(A).** Two massive teeth, situated behind the symphysis of the lower jaw, have produced a formidable appearance in this rare whale. Its body is solid black, sometimes fading to pale gray on the head. Stout and compact in form, with laterally compressed sides, the whale's length is approximately 17 feet (5.2 meters) and its trunk is spindle-shaped, with a triangular dorsal fin rising past the midline of the back, followed by a sharp ridge on the tail stock. Stejneger's beaked whale is found in the North Pacific from the Bering Sea down to California and Japan.

Andrews' Beaked Whale, *Mesoplodon bowdoini.* Measuring up to 15 feet (4.6 meters) in length and very similar in form to *M. carlhubbsi* (it may be a subspecies of *M. carlhubbsi),* this species has a pair of moderately large teeth at the rear of the mandibular symphysis. Considered rare and found only in the South Pacific and the Kerguelen Islands, there is some doubt about its status as a separate species.

True's Beaked Whale, *Mesoplodon mirus* **(B).** In *M. mirus,* the back is dull black, fading to gray on the abdomen. Body length is 16 to 17 feet (4.9 to 5.2 meters), and two massive teeth appear at the tip of the lower jaw in males. Rarely seen, True's beaked whales are found in North Atlantic and South African waters.

Ginkgo-toothed Beaked Whale, *Mesoplodon ginkgodens* **(C).** Spindle-shaped, with some indication of compression, the body of this whale is stout, tapering to a short, heavy caudal section. Its sharp beak contains two teeth, flattened and barely visible, which are behind the mandibular symphysis in the lower jaw of the male. A falcate dorsal fin is placed far down the back, flippers are small, and flukes may have a slight notch on the rear border. Length is approximately 18 feet (5.5 meters). Its body is black, with the underside dark or medium charcoal gray, often covered with white spots or weblike streaks that may be caused by parasites. *M. ginkgodens* is usually located in the southwestern area of the North Pacific, with one stranded specimen found at Del Mar, California.

Hubbs' Beaked Whale, *Mesoplodon carlhubbsi* **(D).** The body of *M. carlhubbsi* is compressed and stout, with small flippers and unnotched flukes. Maximum length is 17 feet (5.2 meters). Color is limited to dark gray or black on the back and sides, fading to a slightly lighter shade on the lower sides and undersurface. Its beak is white or pale gray, with a small white area marking the forehead, and random streaks or spots of pale gray sometimes appearing on its dark back. Two extremely large, flat teeth are behind the symphysis of the lower jaw in the male. Hubbs' beaked whales are confined to the deeper offshore waters of temperate regions from California to British Columbia, in the eastern section of the North Pacific, and the deep waters near Japan, in the western section.

Species of *Mesoplodon:* from top, Stejneger's beaked whale, *M. stejnegeri;* True's beaked whale, *M. mirus;* ginkgo-toothed beaked whale, *M. ginkgodens;* Hubbs' beaked whale, *M. carlhubbsi.*

Battle between two male Cuvier's beaked whales.

Cuvier's Beaked Whale
Ziphius cavirostris

In 1804, the skull of an unknown whale was discovered on the Mediterranean shore of France. Solid and stonelike, it was found to be similar in construction to the ancient skulls of certain mysterious whales excavated in the Netherlands. The relic was listed as a fossil and forgotten until 1850, when a second skull was recovered from the same Mediterranean location. Soon thereafter, a whale with identical skull structure washed up on the shore of New Zealand and caused some dismay among cetologists because it was light above and dark below, a complete reversal of normal whale coloring. It proved to be the rare Cuvier's beaked whale, *Ziphius cavirostris*.

The head of this whale is moderately small, showing a slightly concave profile, with a very short lip line. The body is thickset, with a falcate dorsal fin placed well below the midpoint of the back, and a rather short caudal section surmounted by a well-defined dorsal ridge. The flippers are small, and the flukes do not have a notch. Males attain a length of 18 to 20 feet (5.4 to 6.1 meters), while females reach 20 to 26 feet (6.1 to 8 meters) and may range up to more than 10,000 pounds (4,500 kilograms) in weight. At birth, young whales measure from 6.5 to 10 feet (2 to 3 meters) in length.

There are extreme variations in color. A young female from New Zealand and a male from the Irish coast were described as cream-white on the head, lower jaw, neck, and across the back up to the dorsal fin, with the rest of the body a deep, somber black. Another record listed an aged female as bluish black with a random pattern of white or cream spots on the upper body and solid gray-white on the abdomen. In other variations, the body may be slate gray, bisque, or deep rust brown above and covered with light splotches below, while the back and sides are marked by irregular white lines that appear to be battle scars made by two teeth projecting from the tip of an adult male's lower jaw.

In offshore waters, Cuvier's beaked whales gather in groups of three to twenty-five and travel in rather close contact, diving deep to search the dark, furrowed continental shelf for food. Although *Ziphius* may sample crabs, starfish, and even the lowly sea cucumber, most of its hunting is for squid, other types of cephalopods, and deep-sea fish.

Worldwide in distribution, Cuvier's beaked whales are found near Japan, both coasts of North America and South America, Sweden, England, France, Spain, Corsica, South Africa, India, Australia, and New Zealand. They venture into the North Sea in the Atlantic and, in the Pacific, roam as far north as the Bering Sea and as far south as the tip of South America.

Known and probable range of *Ziphius cavirostris*.

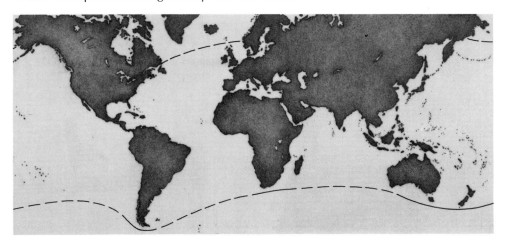

Beaked whales: from top, Shepherd's beaked whale, Baird's beaked whale, and the northern bottlenose whale.

Beaked Whales, Ziphiidae (continued)

SHEPHERD'S BEAKED WHALE
OTHER COMMON NAME: Tasmanian beaked whale
GENUS: *Tasmacetus*
SPECIES: Shepherd's beaked whale, *Tasmacetus shepherdi,* the single species

BAIRD'S BEAKED WHALE
OTHER COMMON NAMES: giant bottlenose whale, Pacific beaked whale
GENUS: *Berardius*
SPECIES: There are two species of the genus *Berardius:*
   Baird's beaked whale, *Berardius bairdii*
   Arnoux's beaked whale, *Berardius arnuxii*

NORTHERN BOTTLENOSE WHALE
OTHER COMMON NAME: none
GENUS: *Hyperoodon*
SPECIES: The genus *Hyperoodon* contains two species:
   Northern bottlenose whale, *Hyperoodon ampullatus*
   Southern bottlenose whale, *Hyperoodon planifrons*

A few stranded whales are the only evidence that Shepherd's beaked whale exists somewhere in the southern oceans.

Shepherd's Beaked Whale
Tasmacetus shepherdi

In February 1973, a stranded whale was sighted on the north side of Península Valdés, in the province of Chubut, Argentina. It was a fortunate discovery, because the body proved to be a specimen of the very rare and seldom seen Shepherd's beaked whale, *Tasmacetus shepherdi.* Two cetologists, James Mead and Roger Payne, immediately went to the site of discovery and began the difficult procedure of a thorough examination.

The body of the whale had washed ashore on a rough, windswept beach in a remote area of the peninsula. Death had apparently occurred one week prior to discovery, and the relatively undamaged condition of the body indicated it had not been long on the beach. Some degree of deterioration had set in, but critically important measurements were taken, an examination was made, and a series of detailed reports on internal organs, and other physical data, were recorded.

The whale was an adult female measuring 22 feet (6.6 meters) in length, with a moderately stout, spindle-shaped body form. A falcate dorsal fin was situated well past the midpoint of the back, flippers were small and narrow, ending in a pointed tip, and the flukes, although damaged, appeared to be rather straight on both anterior and posterior borders, with no indication of a notch. One interesting feature was a sharply pointed beak and the absence of any trace of the two large teeth that are often observed in the lower jaw of most male ziphiids. Not until X-ray plates of the lower jaw were developed did the outline of these two teeth become visible, buried deep within the gums. The rising curve of the melon (or forehead) was comparable to that of Cuvier's beaked whale, but smaller than either the Baird's or the bottlenose whale. Its eyes were larger than those of other ziphiids, and the head, de-

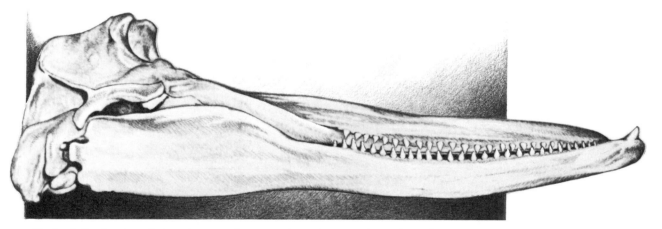

Skull of *T. shepherdi* showing two large teeth and rows of small teeth in upper and lower jaws.

Shepherd's beaked whale (after a drawing by James G. Mead). Details include body form, flipper, dorsal fin, throat grooves, and profile of head.

scribed as bulbous or rounded, narrowed abruptly as the forehead sloped down to a moderately short beak with a projecting lower jaw. On the underside of the throat, two short linear grooves formed an inverted V.

When a whale dies, there is a subtle alteration in color, a loss of delicate shades or pastel undertones as the body gradually darkens until it becomes a dull gray or somber black. On the stranded female, color was difficult to establish, because decomposition had occurred to some degree, but traces of the original pigmentation could be found and compared with the past documentation of other specimens. In this whale, the back was dark, with a very faint indication of the lateral striping described by Oliver (1937) as black dorsally, striped with grayish yellow laterally and white ventrally. Other possible light areas were indicated above the flippers and on top of the head. Past reports, based on personal observation, described the upper part of the whale's body as black with the sides showing streaks or irregular spots of yellow or grayish yellow that faded to pale ivory or pure white on the underside. This description coincided with the very faint indication of a striping pattern on the Península Valdés whale.

Tasmacetus differed from all other beaked whales in having an unusually straight lip line and a sharply pointed beak containing approximately 90 small teeth, with 17 to 21 teeth in each side of the upper jaw and 22 to 28 teeth in each side of the lower jaw. Also, projecting from the tip of the lower jaw and completely concealed within the gums were two very large teeth with broad bases and conical crowns. It should be noted that, among the confirmed specimens of *T. shepherdi,* the number of teeth varied, and since the small teeth were described by one expert as showing obvious signs of wear, they were considered to be functional.

A considerable number of bottom fishes had been consumed, and the remains of a crab and a squid were identified, but were considered doubtful because they might have been inside the bottom-feeding fish. The whale had fed principally on hake, usually found near the ocean floor to a depth of 2,500 feet (750 meters), suggesting these whales feed near the bottom in very deep water.

The stranded specimen on the coast of Argentina has now extended the known area of Shepherd's beaked whale, usually found near New Zealand, and indicates a possible range throughout the oceans of the southern hemisphere.

Known and theoretical range of Shepherd's beaked whale in the southern hemisphere.

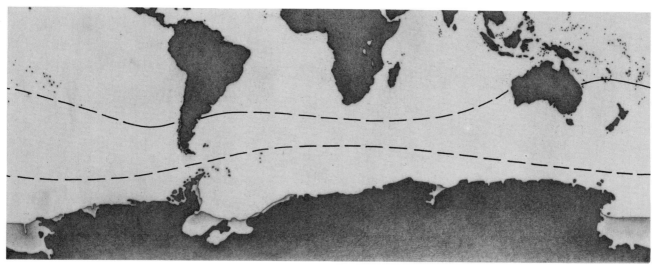

Baird's beaked whales are often called the "giant bottlenose whales."

Baird's Beaked Whale
Berardius bairdii

Baird's beaked whale, *Berardius bairdii,* patrols the deeper offshore areas of the North Pacific, gliding through blue-black water where light filters dimly from above to touch the great, ghostly forms with eerie luster. Long-bodied and slender, Baird's whale is one of the largest ziphiids, or beaked whales, ranging from 32 to 34 feet (9.8 to 10.5 meters) in length, with females reaching a maximum of 42 feet (12.8 meters) and males 39 feet (11.8 meters). It is sometimes called the "giant bottlenose whale."

Externally, the tapered beak and high forehead of *Berardius* are somewhat similar to those of the famed bottlenose whale *Hyperoodon ampullatus.* Two pairs of teeth, the front ones of massive size, are situated at the tip of a projecting lower jaw, and the throat is marked by two large grooves that form an inverted V. Well past the midpoint of the back there is a triangular dorsal fin with a straight posterior margin; the flippers are small, but the flukes are very wide. All of the upper body, including flippers and flukes, is a dark bluish gray or brownish black, becoming a lighter gray on the underside, with a network of narrow white scars carved by a rival's teeth marking the back, and a few scattered white spots on the abdomen.

A pelagic, or deep-sea, species seldom approaching any shores, *Berardius* prefers to travel in schools of six to thirty whales, either limited to males, or possibly females led by a large male, all moving in such close proximity that flukes and flippers often touch as they sweep downward into darkness around 3,300 feet (1,000 meters) to probe the enveloping gloom for squid. At higher levels, they pursue schools of herring and follow the sepia trails of octopuses. In relatively shallow waters, they snatch up crabs and eat such unlikely oddities as starfish, sea cucumbers, and bulbous sea squirts. When alarmed, these shy whales become alert and fast-moving, diving at a steep angle and remaining down for approximately one hour.

In the eastern North Pacific, Baird's beaked whales range from Lower California to the Bering Strait in Alaska, and in the western North Pacific, they migrate from the Okhotsk Sea down to southeastern Japan. After reaching these warmer waters, breeding occurs from November through May. According to reports, there is a gestation period of approximately twelve months, followed by the birth of calves measuring around 15 feet (4.5 meters) in length.

Arnoux's beaked whale, *Berardius arnuxii,* the southern species, has a shorter length of 29.5 feet (9 meters), while its head, flippers and flukes are larger than those of *B. bairdii.* The back is dark blue, changing to mottled blue-gray sides and a gray abdomen. The southern whale has been reported near Australia, New Zealand, the Falkland Islands, South Africa, South Georgia Island, and the South Shetland Islands, indicating a range worldwide in the southern hemisphere, possibly limited to temperate waters.

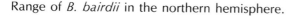

Range of *B. bairdii* in the northern hemisphere.

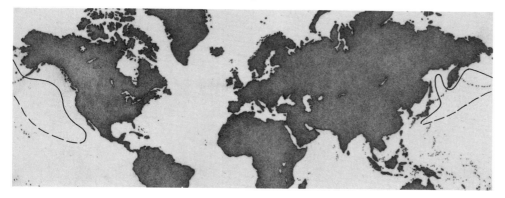

Northern bottlenose whales; young, adult, and aged.

Northern Bottlenose Whale
Hyperoodon ampullatus

The northern bottlenose whale, *Hyperoodon ampullatus,* is named for a very prominent forehead, or melon, that rises abruptly above a short beak. Underlying this melon are outgrowths of the skull in the form of large bony crests which give a bottle-like appearance to the head. In young whales, male and female, these crests are not enlarged and form a low, wide basin on the upper surface of the skull. As the male matures, however, proliferation takes place and the rising crests of bone gradually increase in size until, in old males, the expansion of the maxillary crests produces two knobs of bone so massive that only a narrow slit remains to separate their edges. In females, the area in front of the crests contains a small cavity filled with a colorless oil that is extremely dense. In males, this cavity is packed with an oval mass of solid fat, measuring approximately twice the volume of a large watermelon.

Exceedingly powerful, shaped like a torpedo, the bottlenose is famed for the tremendous speed of its dive and the ability to remain submerged at great depth for one to two hours. Its body is highly streamlined, with a small, sickle-shaped dorsal fin rising on its back beyond the midpoint of the body; the flippers are small and tapered, while the flukes are moderately broad without any indication of a notch. On its lower throat, two short ventral grooves appear in the shape of a V. Like other ziphiids, each male bottlenose whale has two large teeth at the tip of the lower jaw, which usually erupt from the tissues of the gums. In females, the tip of the lower jaw appears toothless but actually contains two teeth that do not emerge from the gums. Apart from these large teeth, there is a report of a female whale with rows of tiny, half-formed teeth, resembling toothpicks, buried deep within the tissues of the gums in both upper and lower jaws.

An adult male *Hyperoodon* reaches a length of around 32 feet (9.8 meters), and an adult female measures approximately 25 feet (7.5 meters). Weight records list a 20-foot (6-meter) female at 5,600 pounds (2,540 kilograms). Color appears to vary according to age. Calves are black or dark brown at birth, turning chocolate brown as they mature, a uniform color that gradually changes as pale spots appear on the flanks and back, coalescing to produce a marbled or splotched effect, while the flippers and flukes remain dark. In older whales, the blackish-brown back and gray underparts often fade until a very old male with a notched and bulging forehead may eventually display a white head, or, rarely, become almost entirely grayish white.

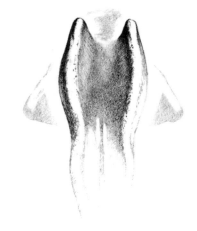

Like the great sperm whale, the bottlenose is a deepwater species requiring more than 4,800 feet (800 fathoms) between the ocean surface and floor. Since these whales feed on several types of squid, with each type found at a specific depth, an examination of the stomach contents of stranded whales has confirmed a regular descent to a depth of 1,500 feet (450 meters). Record dives of two hours have been observed, but regular dives usually require around fifty minutes, with a rest of ten minutes on the surface.

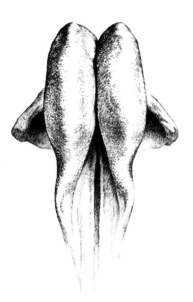

Massive growth of the maxillary crest in a male bottlenose whale.

When preparing to dive, a bottlenose takes several deep breaths, then plunges swiftly downward. At once, major physiological changes begin to take place as its body adjusts to the pressure of increasing depth and a lack of oxygen. In rapid succession, its heartbeat slows and the volume of blood circulating through its body is redistributed, with a large supply of blood being channeled to the whale's brain, heart, and other essential organs. In certain areas, a system of valves, or sphincter muscles, shut off the arteries leading to less important parts of the body, beginning with the flippers, flukes, and caudal section, then the kidneys, intestinal tract, and other organs.

As the pressure of great depth increases, the whale's body begins to draw upon an enormous supply of oxygen retained in great bands of muscle fibers

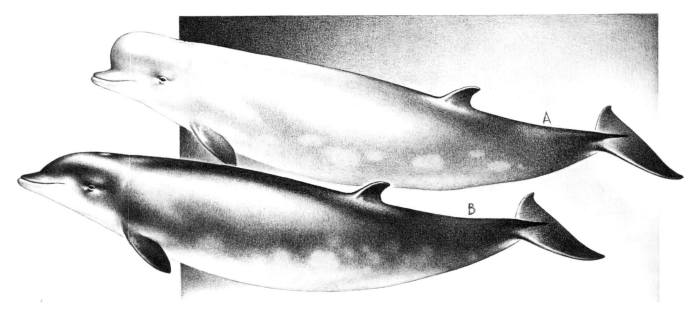

(A) Male and (B) female whales.

by a dark red pigment called myoglobin, or muscle hemoglobin. This iron-bearing substance far surpasses regular hemoglobin in its ability to store oxygen, and it has been estimated (Slijper, 1962) that diving whales carry 41 percent of their oxygen in muscle tissues. This major adaptation allows both the deep-diving bottlenose whale and the great sperm whale to wander at great depth for a very long time without surfacing for a breath of air.

There has been some speculation concerning the purpose of the odd formation of knobs, or bosses, on the forehead of *Hyperoodon.* It has been suggested that the massive enlargement of these maxillary crests may provide acoustic baffles for deflecting sound into a wave guide (Mitchell and Kozicki). Such an accommodation in bottlenose whales may assist in searching the total darkness of the deep-sea bottom, perhaps with a side-swimming motion, as observed in the Ganges susu, to scan for timid octopus and fast-moving squid.

When searching for squid, the whales gather in small groups or, in certain seasons, assemble in herds composed of thousands of males and females of various ages and sizes, usually led by old males. To find food, a group of up to ten whales will descend in close formation, plunging far down through a deepening gloom into echoing darkness, where they follow the darting flight of small, swift cephalopods. If squid are scarce, young herring, krill, and such ocean-floor dwellers as starfish are taken as food.

The range of northern bottlenose whales extends throughout the cold, deep waters of the North Atlantic Ocean. In summer, they advance into frigid waters, going as far north as the white floes and drifting bergs of the Arctic Ocean, the Greenland and Norwegian seas, Cape Chidley, and the Gully, a deep submarine canyon near Sable Island, Nova Scotia. Migrating schools may separate, leaving females and young in one group and males in another, with the older males penetrating very close to the permanent pack ice. In fall, they retreat as far south as Rhode Island, in the western Atlantic, and in the east they pass near England, the Netherlands, France, and the Cape Verde Islands (15° north latitude). In these temperate and tropical waters, the females bear their young, measuring approximately 10 feet (3 meters) in length, in April or May one year after mating. The interval between births is estimated at two to three years.

The southern bottlenose whale, *Hyperoodon planifrons,* a second species which closely resembles the northern bottlenose, is found far to the south. Records list a body length of around 32 feet (9.7 meters) for a male and 24 feet (7.4 meters) for a female. In appearance, the southern bottlenose whale has moderately large flippers and flukes but shows a greater expansion of the forehead and a larger dorsal fin than the northern whale. Color has been described as black or dark grayish brown on the back, changing to a pale brownish gray on the abdomen.

The southern bottlenose is believed to inhabit the chill and turbulent waters that circle Antarctica and has been observed near Australia, New Zealand, Chile, Argentina, the Falkland Islands, South Africa, and the Pacific and Indian oceans.

Range of northern and southern bottlenose whales.

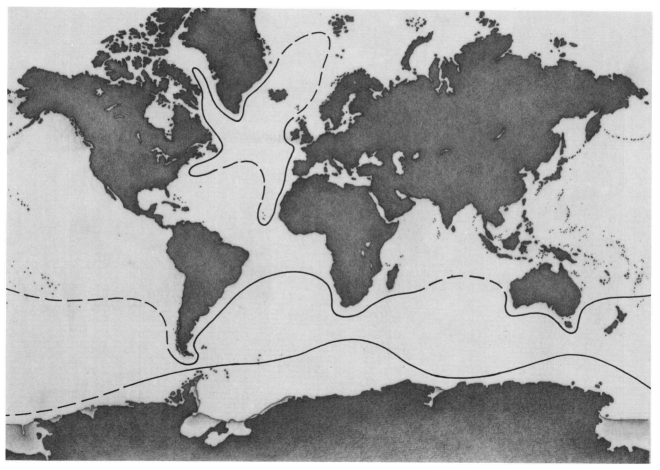

Sperm whales: sperm whale and pygmy sperm whale.

Sperm Whales, Physeteridae

The great sperm whale, *Physeter catodon* (also listed as *Physeter macrocephalus*), shares the family Physeteridae with a pair of very small relatives, virtually unknown and seldom seen, that are listed under the names of pygmy sperm whale, *Kogia breviceps,* and dwarf sperm whale, *Kogia simus.* Among the characteristics identifying the two genera, *Physeter* and *Kogia,* are skulls which have a basin-like structure. The massive skull of *Physeter* is distorted and extends to an extreme length, while the skull of *Kogia* is very short. Both genera produce spermaceti, a glistening oil or waxlike substance retained in a reservoir in the head; both have a slender lower jaw lined with 8 to 25 pairs of functional teeth that fit securely into deep sockets in the upper jaw when the mouth is closed; and both have a spine in which most of the cervical vertebrae are fused.

Apart from these similarities, *Physeter* and *Kogia* bear little resemblance to each other in body form, size, and temperament. The great sperm whale, with its massive head, wrinkled skin, and powerful body ranging up to 61 feet (18.5 meters) in length, has a formidable appearance and a well-deserved reputation as a warrior. The shy little pygmy and dwarf sperm whales are more dolphinlike in form and measure a mere 11 feet (3.4 meters) and 8.8 feet (2.7 meters), respectively.

Listed below are the sperm whales, their common names, classifications, and numbers of species.

SPERM WHALE
OTHER COMMON NAME: cachalot
GENUS: *Physeter*
SPECIES: sperm whale, *Physeter catodon,* the single species

PYGMY SPERM WHALE
OTHER COMMON NAMES: lesser sperm whale, lesser cachalot, short-headed sperm whale
GENUS: *Kogia*
SPECIES: There are two species in the genus *Kogia:*
Pygmy sperm whale, *Kogia breviceps*
Dwarf sperm whale, *Kogia simus*

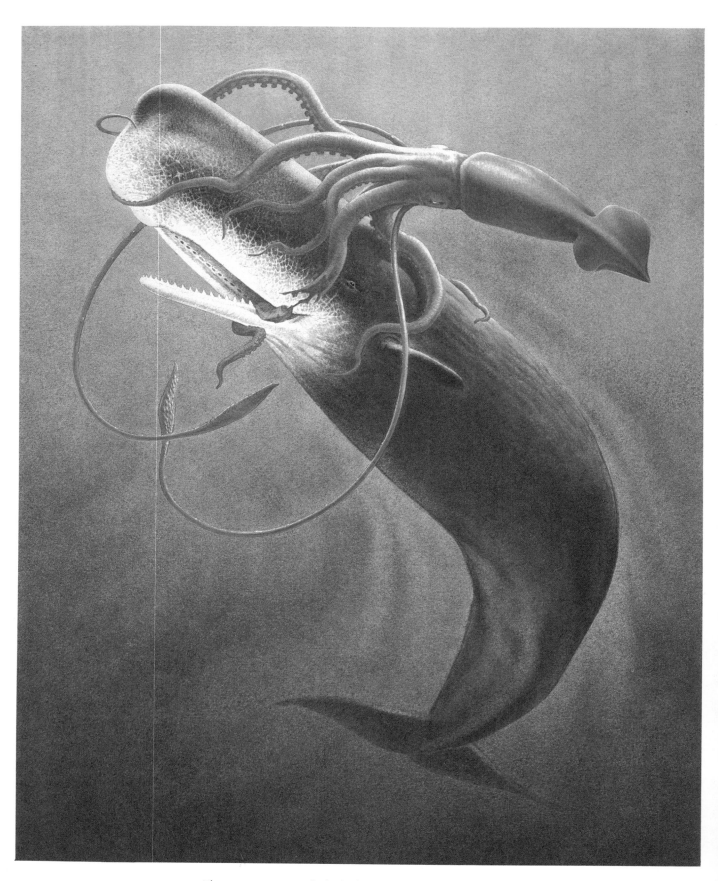

The great sperm whale locked in battle with a giant squid.

Sperm Whale
Physeter catodon

When the great sperm whale, *Physeter catodon,* prepares to descend to the bottom of the sea, his back curves into a tight arc and the broad flukes of his tail swing high into the air, then slip slowly beneath the surface of cool, blue-green water, leaving a trail of silver bubbles. At a near-vertical incline, the powerful black form glides downward, moving lower and lower through a subdued green light that gradually changes to blue, then deepens to a dark indigo. At 330 feet (100 meters), the whale's body adjusts to an increase in pressure and the coldness of the water. Blood begins to retreat from his flukes, flippers, and the outer part of his body, concentrating in vital organs and his immense brain (the largest one on earth). At this point, his heart, almost 6.5 feet (2 meters) wide, is constricted, its beat falling to 10 percent of normal.

Far down now, the faint blue-black light merges into pitch black as the whale passes below 1,600 feet (500 meters), then 3,300 feet (1,000 meters), steadily plunging deeper and deeper until he finally reaches the crushing depth of 4,000 feet (1,200 meters). Here he levels out, his lower jaw close to the ocean floor. For half an hour, moving in total darkness through near-freezing water under an awesome pressure of 120 atmospheres, the old warrior prowls the barren terrain of the bottom, emitting a barrage of sharp clicks, searching for an echo of his deadly foe, the giant squid *Architeuthis.*

Sperm whales are built on a massive scale, with body length at times reaching 60.6 feet (18.5 meters). The heavy flukes span 13 to 15 feet (4 to 4.5 meters) in width, rounded flippers are relatively small, and the skin of the body has irregular furrows with deep folds around the throat. In place of a dorsal fin, there is a large hump, followed by a row of smaller bumps on the dorsal ridge. Shaped like a blunt-nosed missile, the body tapers backward to the base of the tail and narrows slightly forward along the great rounded barrel of the head.

Comprising one fourth to almost one third of its total length, the enormous head of a sperm whale is peculiar in construction. The floor of the skull is broadly flat, projecting forward to a pointed tip and rising concavely on either side in back to form a solid, basin-like support for a huge, rectangular reservoir, or tank. The lower part of this tank contains an oily residue, or "junk," while the upper part holds an immense hollow case. There is a large air sac behind the case and another in front, which may act as sound reflectors. The right nasal tube runs under the case and ends in a pair of dark liplike forms, called the *museau du singe* (monkey's muzzle), that open into the front air sac. The left breathing tube rises on the left side to open into a single blowhole.

The great hollow case above the residue tank is filled with a strange liquid, a glistening, colorless substance called "spermaceti." In very deep, cold wa-

The black form plunges downward at a nearly vertical angle.

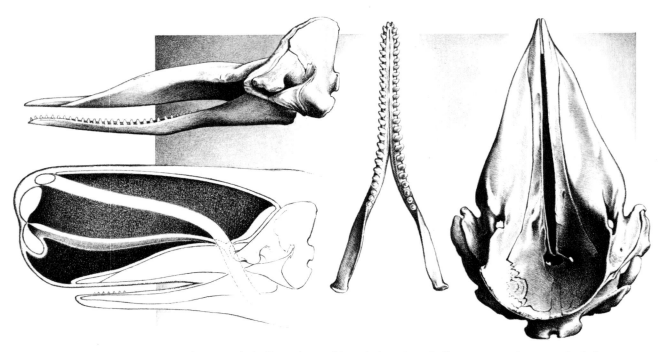

Lateral view of skull; outline of head showing skull, spermaceti reservoir, left breathing tube, and two air sacs; dorsal view of the lower jaw; and dorsal view of the great, basin-like skull (after Howell).

ter, this clear oil solidifies into a soft, white wax. Its function is not clearly understood, but recent discoveries indicate that spemaceti can absorb almost six times more nitrogen than whale blood can, thus preventing a heavy formation of nitrogen bubbles when surfacing from deep dives. It may also act as a buoyancy regulator, cooling into a heavy wax to counteract the buoyancy that develops as water density increases at great depths. Thus the sperm whale would remain normally buoyant at any depth. Below this vast, barrel-like nose, the lower jaw appears very narrow and fragile. It is a powerful weapon, however, armed with 18 to 25 strong, conical teeth on each side. In the upper jaw, there are matching rows of horny sheaths, or holes, into which the teeth fit when the mouth is closed. This upper jaw sometimes contains very small teeth buried deep within the gums. The entire surface of the tongue is pale, and the interior of the mouth is a luminous white. It has been suggested that, in the blackness of lower depths, this brilliant white skin acts as a lure to entice squid within reach of the crushing lower jaw.

Sperm whales are rusty black or a very deep indigo gray. Individual variation is apparent in a piebald spotting or clusters of semi-white streaks near the navel and the anus. Long streaks and circles of white scar tissue, caused by the suckers of giant squid, ornament the entire head and radiate from the shining white skin surrounding the mouth. Calves are blackish gray when born, becoming darker as adults, then developing irregular gray-white areas with advancing age. Pure white individuals are very rare.

In oceans throughout the world, between 70° north and 70° south latitude, the main hunting grounds of these great whales are situated in waters well

Dorsal and ventral views of a female sperm whale.

below 650 feet (200 meters), more often in deep areas of the sea, where small groups cruise in total darkness, traveling through currents that bring a wide variety of squid, fish, and other favorite foods to their open jaws. In regions where there is a confluence of cold currents merging with warm, tropical waters, such as the Humboldt Current, near Chile and Peru, and the Benguela Current, off southwestern Africa, great herds collect to feed on teeming masses of squid that thrive in these tumultuous convergences.

Requiring a ton of food a day, each whale seeks not only heavy concentrations of squid, but also schools of larger fish such as cod, barracuda, ray, and albacore, along with a few seals and any sharks measuring up to 10 feet (3 meters). Apart from this regular fare, there is evidence that some whales may sample very strange items. Stomach contents have contained pieces of wood, stones of all sizes, and coconuts still encased in their heavy outer shells. There are also records of an occasional whale with one third of its first stomach filled with sand.

Of all the prey mighty *Physeter* pursues, no other creatures are so wrapped in an aura of mystery and legend as are giant squids of the genus *Architeuthis*. They are the kraken of ancient folklore, the fabled monsters of the deep that preyed on ships in bygone days and brought terror to those who sailed the seas. Estimated to attain a length of 30 to 56 feet (9 to 17 meters), with a thick, rounded body and winged tail, *Architeuthis* is equipped with eight arms lined with suction disks and two long, whiplike tentacles. In search of this nightmarish beast, the sperm whale stalks his prey from moderate depths down into the blackness of abyssal zones and often bears the scars of violent battles fought with these powerful cephalopods.

One of the mysteries surrounding sperm whales is the formation of a very rare and exotic substance called ambergris. It was thought that extensive feeding on squid, combined with a difficulty in digesting their parrotlike beaks, caused an accumulation of horny material in the lower intestinal tract of the whale. Research has recently indicated, however, that while squid beaks are usually present in the material, at other times there is no trace of them. The chemical process by which this unique compound is formed is unknown. Formerly used as a stabilizer of floral essences in the finest perfumes, it is now replaced by synthetic preparations.

There is a marked difference in the size of male and female whales. Males are large, measuring from 50.5 feet (15.4 meters) up to 62 feet (19 meters), with a weight of 35 to over 51 tons (32,000 to over 46,000 kilograms), while females are relatively small, seldom exceeding 38 feet (11.6 meters) and a weight of 18 tons (16,000 kilograms). There is also a difference in range. Throughout the year, female sperm whales are found in temperate waters, always within 30° to 50° latitude north and south. Lingering in this area, dominant bulls attach themselves to herds of cows and remain to guard them, while other males form carefree bachelor groups and wander far up into the North Atlantic and the Bering Sea, in the northern hemisphere, or the South Shetland Islands, near Antarctica, in the southern hemisphere.

In winter, these wide-ranging companies and solitary roving males return once more to warm waters to follow in the wake of loosely knit herds composed of cows, calves, and immature young whales shepherded by large,

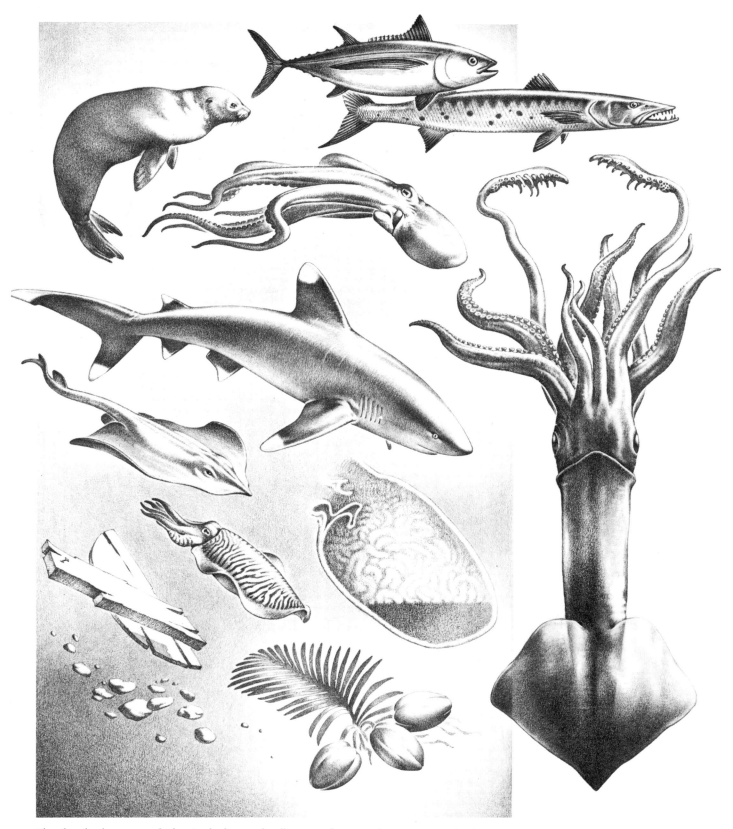

The food of sperm whales includes seal, albacore, barracuda, octopus, shark, skate, cuttlefish, squid, and such odd items as random pieces of wood, stones, coconuts, and sand (sometimes filling a whale's forestomach to 1/3 capacity).

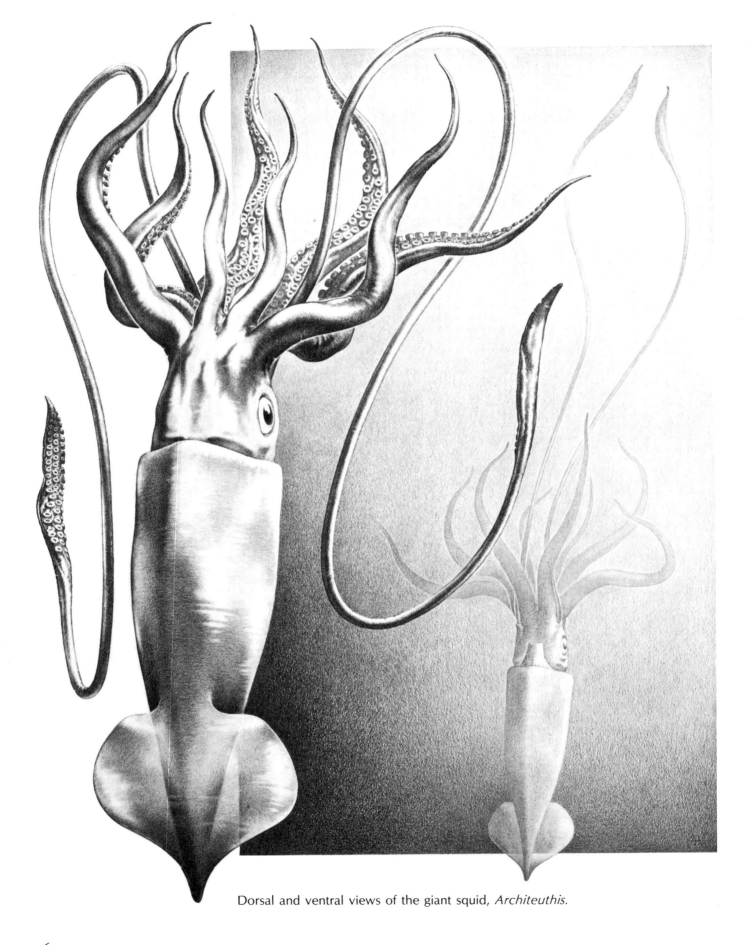

Dorsal and ventral views of the giant squid, *Architeuthis*.

battle-scarred bulls. As these random groups merge, the assembly increases to very large mixed herds that include young mature males and older, stronger bulls. By late winter, the combination has become explosive.

When a powerful male leaves the lagging bachelor group and advances to challenge a harem master, open warfare erupts. Seething with fury, the harem bull plunges forward to meet his opponent's charge, striking the other whale with brutal force as they ram head on, then withdraw to repeat the bone-jarring impact, time after time. Rolling onto their backs, lower jaws extended at a 90° angle, the whales charge forward and spar briefly, their lower jaws snapping viciously until one locks on the other in a twisted, vise-like grip that can crack a brittle jawbone and bring the battle to an abrupt end. Many males, when defeated and injured, separate from the herd and lead the solitary life of a wanderer.

Schools of female sperm whales are unusually stable, with many whales remaining for years and possibly for life within the same school. It is to these maternal family groups that the wandering males return during the eight months of the breeding season. Among incoming whales, tension rises as they approach their destination and the ritual of courtship begins to reach a climax. High-strung and eager, many males seek to attract the attention of females with flipper touches, posturing, and short, sinuous chases, all of these enticements finally winding up to a rapping of heads, a locking of jaws, and a sudden, swift mating. In summer, after a period of sixteen months, each mother whale gives birth to a single calf, 11 to 14 feet (3.5 to 4.5 meters) long. Carefully tended by older members of the herd and guarded by the great warrior bulls, the young whale remains close to its mother until it has learned to feed itself by diving down to the middle depths to pursue small, diaphanous squid and schools of silvery fish.

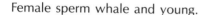
Female sperm whale and young.

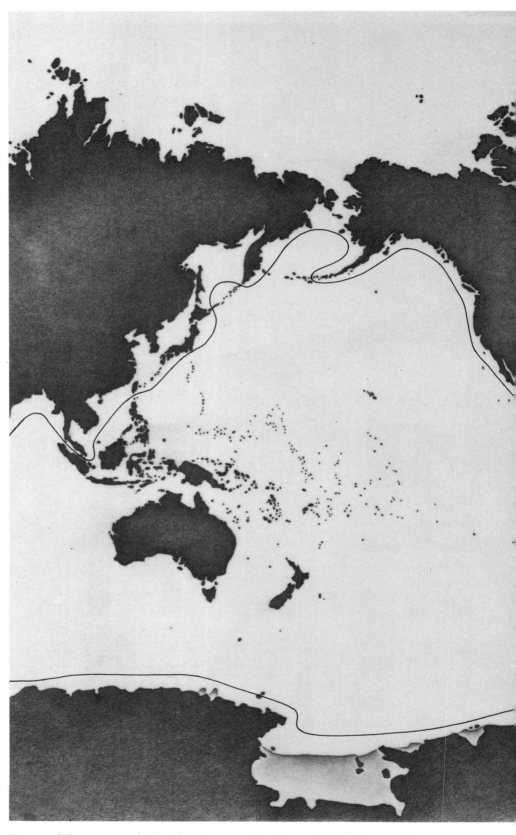

Range of the sperm whale, *Physeter catodon,* is worldwide in very deep waters.

Slow and placid, a pygmy sperm whale is no match for playful fur seals.

Pygmy Sperm Whale
Kogia breviceps

The only living relatives of the great sperm whale, *Physeter catodon,* are two comparatively unknown whales of diminutive size and solitary habits called the pygmy sperm whale, *Kogia breviceps,* and the dwarf sperm whale, *Kogia simus.* The pattern of their daily lives has remained something of a mystery; nevertheless, a limited amount of information, gathered from stranded specimens and a few living whales, has provided some knowledge concerning the structure, color, distribution, and habits of these shy little whales.

The pygmy sperm whale, *K. breviceps,* is short and plump, reaching a maximum length of approximately 11 feet (3.4 meters) and a weight ranging up to a hefty 900 pounds (400 kilograms), with male and female of equal size. Situated beyond the midline of the body, the dorsal fin is small and falcate, flippers are wide with a rounded point, flukes are large, and the caudal section is compressed laterally, being half as wide as it is high. Color ranges from black to dark brownish gray on the back, gray on the sides, fading to grayish white on the underside, with the flippers described as slate gray on top but lighter below, and the flukes listed as a dark uniform gray.

In contrast to the immense head of its huge relative, the head of *K. breviceps,* which contains a little spermaceti reservoir, is small and is considered remarkable in structure. Among the many peculiarities reported is the discovery that the mandible, or lower jaw, is incredibly thin and appears to be quite fragile. Blunt and high, the small whale's snout projects well beyond the lower jaw, with a single blowhole opening on top of the head and a white mark, or false gill, appearing below the ear opening. Its mouth, surprisingly small, narrow, and sharklike in form, contains 12 to 16 pairs of thin, curved, sharply pointed teeth. One interesting account states that these teeth, which line the sides of the lower jaw and fit snugly into round sockets in the upper jaw, actually resemble the teeth of a large python.

Instead of traveling in the security of a sociable group of companions, a pygmy sperm whale often seems to shun the company of its own kind, making its solitary way through the cool, quiet depths of the ocean along unknown migratory routes. Slow in movement and placid in temperament, the little whale apparently has no defense in an encounter with a pack of killer whales; nor is it a match for spirited dolphins, or for wandering bands of playful fur seals that, in passing, may surround it with a swirling confusion of graceful forms. When tired, it has a habit of resting on the surface in a

Skull and lower jaw of a pygmy sperm whale (upper) and dwarf sperm whale (lower).

Pygmy sperm whale (right) and dwarf sperm whale (left).

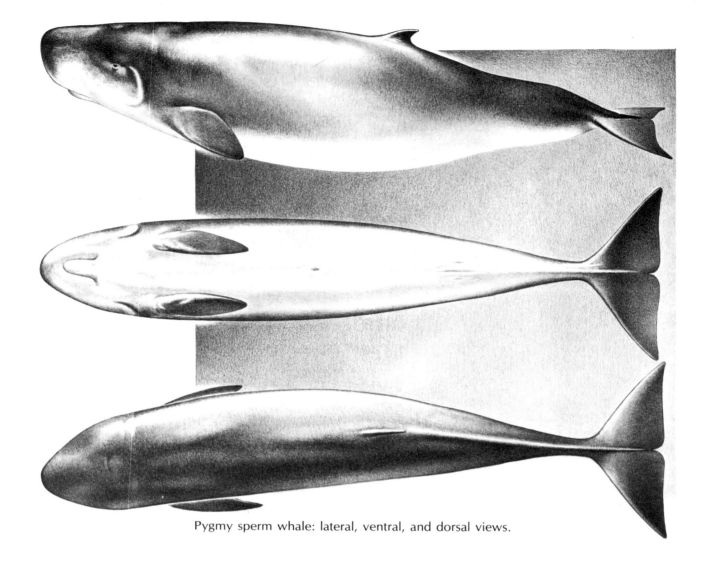

Pygmy sperm whale: lateral, ventral, and dorsal views.

manner reminiscent of its great relative. It lies motionless, its blowhole above water level and its body slanting downward with the tail hanging slack. The great sperm whale often naps in this position, sinking into a sleep so profound that ships have collided head on with the slumbering giant, sometimes with considerable damage to both ship and whale.

In certain seasons, pygmy sperm whales may gather in very small groups consisting of three to six individuals to pursue pelagic squid and fish, or wander along the continental shelf in search of marine crabs, scuttling shore crabs, and shrimps. There is some indication the whales may migrate toward colder regions in summer, traveling as far north as the chill waters of the Labrador Current near Nova Scotia and, in the eastern Atlantic, venturing into the restless North Sea near the Netherlands. At the first touch of winter's cold, however, they return to warmer climates, with some individuals retreating southward as far as the southern extremity of South America, South Africa, and Tasmania, ocean areas that overlap the range of *Kogia simus,* the dwarf sperm whale. Among the very few accounts of the delivery of an infant pygmy sperm whale, there was one that took place in November, when a 10-foot (3-meter) adult female gave birth, while stranded, to a 6-foot (1.75-meter) calf.

The range of these small whales appears to be worldwide, with a record of stranded individuals collected from the Netherlands, France, Japan, Portugal, and both coasts of North America. In the southern hemisphere, they appear to prefer ocean areas around New Zealand and southeastern Australia. Like the great sperm whale, little *Kogia breviceps* is widely distributed in the North Pacific and the North Atlantic, advancing into higher latitudes than *K. simus.*

The dwarf sperm whale, *Kogia simus,* closely resembles the pygmy sperm whale in appearance, having a similar, but smaller, blunt head, a pale mark, or false gill, below the ear orifice, and a stout body form. It is much shorter than *K. breviceps,* however, ranging from 7 to 9 feet (2.1 to 2.7 meters), and its dorsal fin is higher and more centrally located, like the prominent fin of a bottlenose dolphin. On its throat, there are a few shallow grooves shaped like the short throat furrows of a sperm whale, and its lower jaw, small and exceedingly narrow, is lined with eight to eleven pairs of curved, needlelike teeth. Color is limited to dark gray on top, fading to pale gray on the sides, then changing to grayish white below.

Although the dwarf sperm whale has been recognized as a separate species and given a different name, records of its habits and territory unfortunately are confused with those of its congener, *K. breviceps.* While the two species are often found in the same area and freely mix, the dwarf sperm whale, *K. simus,* appears to prefer southern latitudes but is not restricted to the southern hemisphere. Stranded whales have been found on the shores of South Africa, India, Indochina, Australia, New Zealand, Japan, California, Florida, and North Carolina.

Theoretical range of *K. breviceps* and *K. simus.*

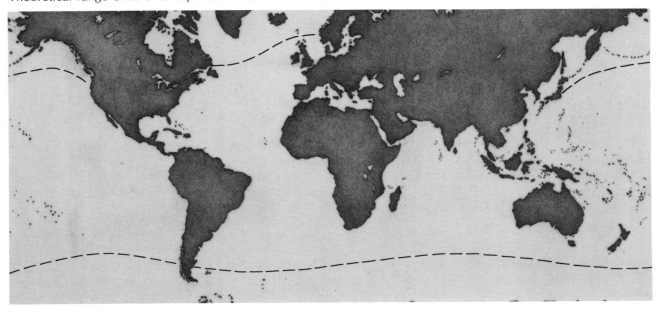

Arctic whales, white whale (above) and narwhal (below).

Arctic Whales, Monodontidae

The icebound coastal areas and chill waters of the Arctic are the home of two whales that have fascinated man since the Middle Ages; they are the legendary white whale, or beluga, and the narwhal. Because they are unique, these beautiful whales have been placed in a separate family called the Monodontidae and can be identified by some remarkable features.

The fame of the narwhal comes from the growth of a long spiral tusk extending outward from its left upper jaw. The beluga is recognized worldwide for its vocal ability and gleaming white skin. Actually, both whales are white, cream, or grayish white, but in the narwhal, this basic body color is overlaid with an intricate pattern of random spots and streaks of black or brownish gray. Both are moderate in size, with a beakless head and a very robust body. In place of a dorsal fin, a low ridge rises midway on the back, the flippers are rounded, and the flukes have a circular, fanlike shape indented by a definite notch. The first two cervical vertebrae are fused, while all other vertebrae are separate and appear to move with the same ease as those of river dolphins.

No common name accompanies the listing of the family Monodontidae (similar to the term "river dolphins" for Platanistidae or "beaked whales" for Ziphiidae); therefore the term "arctic whales" was selected as an appropriate common name but is not in general use at this time.

Listed below are the two whales, their common names, classifications, and species.

WHITE WHALE
   OTHER COMMON NAMES: beluga, belukha, white porpoise, sea canary
   GENUS: *Delphinapterus*
   SPECIES: white whale, *Delphinapterus leucas,* the single species

NARWHAL
   OTHER COMMON NAMES: narwhale, unicorn whale (historical name)
   GENUS: *Monodon*
   SPECIES: narwhal, *Monodon monoceros,* the single species

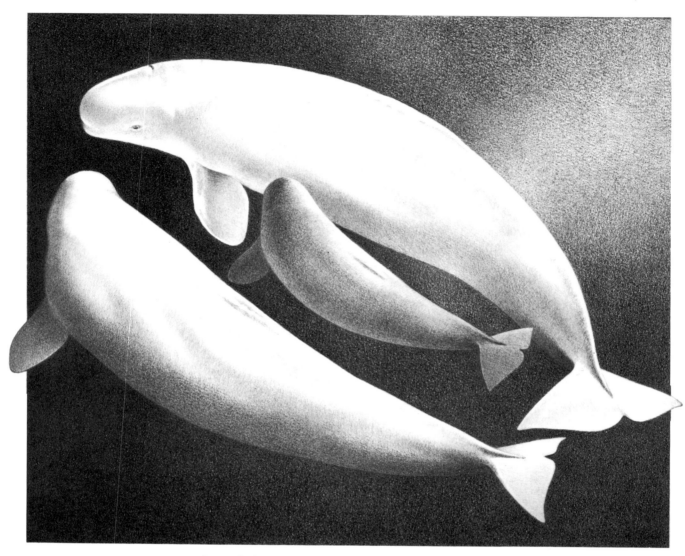

White whales in the dark waters of the Arctic Ocean.

White Whale
Delphinapterus leucas

Surrounded by a soft translucence of blue-green light filtering down through polished layers of ice, the white whale, or beluga, *Delphinapterus leucas,* is a very beautiful creature, gleaming white against the dark waters of the Arctic Ocean, its rounded form showing no mark or tint of pigment to mar the immaculate whiteness of its skin. Even the mouth and tongue are without color, and only its eyes, black and bright, contrast in brilliance.

Viewed from any angle, the body of a white whale is extremely robust, ranging up to 2,400 pounds (1,100 kilograms) and around 16 feet (5 meters) in length, with males measuring slightly larger than females. In place of a dorsal fin, there is a short, low ridge rising midway on the whale's back; its flippers have a broad paddle shape, and the flukes are convex, showing an unusual fanlike curve on the posterior border. The head is round and beakless, with 8 to 11 strong teeth lining each side of the upper jaw and 8 to 9 teeth in each side of the lower jaw.

Belugas are coast-loving whales, prone to wander along familiar shorelines in small groups, at times gathering in large mixed companies of males and females, numbering up to two hundred whales, that explore the sunlit areas where schools of small herring streak the bright green water with silver and young flatfish collect in sandy hollows until chased out by the whales. Seldom diving deeper than 50 feet (15 meters), they probe among layered rocks for shrimps and lobsters, or glide down to examine narrow crevices and clumps of seaweed where small, elusive crabs could hide. In deeper waters, they scan the depths for arctic cod, a favorite food, or linger near a broad river estuary to intercept and feast on salmon returning from the sea to spawn. These migrating schools of fish are often followed by a horde of predators that may include enemies of the white whales.

Of all the sounds echoing through the ocean, none are more feared than the rhythmic movements of orcas, or killer whales. Even when warned by heavy vibrations, white whales are not swift enough to outdistance a pack of these hunters; therefore, when danger is near, the whales will enter a broad marsh area or seek concealment in the heavy slush between ice floes or the alcoves in subterranean layers of the pack ice. If killer whales appear suddenly in the vicinity of belugas, they will become motionless white forms

Belugas are robust in form.

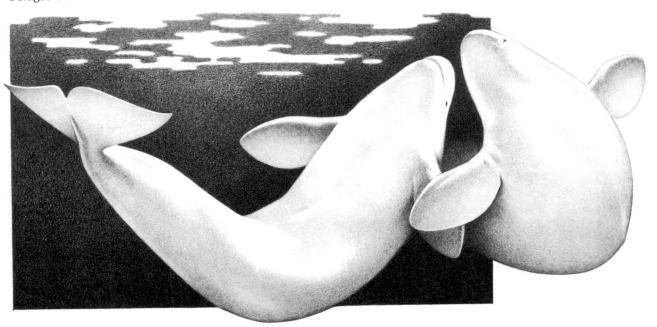

Polar bear waiting near a breathing hole.

among broken ice slabs, with no sound to betray their presence—a strategy that often allows them to escape the notice of hungry orcas.

In September, as the sun moves lower on the horizon, the short arctic summer quickly fades, and small groups of white whales reluctantly turn from ice-coated shorelines to begin their migration south. In severe winters, rapidly forming ice may block the shallow opening of a deep bay or inlet, imprisoning the belugas. As the surface begins to freeze over, the whales, trapped beneath a deepening layer of ice, are forced to maintain breathing holes in the thickening ice shield, pressing around the small opening of the hole to snatch a breath until overcome by weakness, or, as sometimes happens, until they fall prey to a land-base hunter of unusual skill and patience.

The coming of winter's cold and darkness does not find the Arctic silent or empty of life. Prowling over hummocks and hunting along the frozen shorelines, male polar bears patrol the edge of the ice, searching for the form of a sleeping seal, or the dark circle of a breathing hole in the limitless white landscape. When the powerful beast locates a fresh hole, it stretches out beside the opening and waits, one foreleg extended to land a crushing blow on the head of a seal or a desperate whale as it rises to breathe, killing it instantly. The body is then dragged out onto the ice away from the dark opening. According to one account, more than thirteen white whales have been killed at a single breathing hole and dragged behind a ridge by an excited bear.

Most of the whales move into the warmth of open waters where they pass the rigors of the icebound months until spring, when large numbers assemble in the shelter of warm bays or major rivers, such as western Hudson Bay, Lancaster Sound, and the St. Lawrence River, to participate in the ritual of courtship. From June to August, many of the females withdraw to secluded areas to give birth, after a long gestation, to a small gray calf. Among belugas, a mother whale is attended by a young female, a devoted companion and nurse able to assist in the delivery and in caring for the infant.

The body of a newborn beluga measures approximately 5 feet (1.5 meters) and is creased with the vertical lines of deeply indented fetal folds. Nature has provided the infant with ample time to develop, allowing a mother beluga to carry her unborn young for a period of fourteen months before giving birth in the cold waters of northern latitudes. After the newborn has drawn a series of experimental breaths, the mother rests on her side near the surface and waits until the infant instinctively finds two vertical slits on her caudal section. Inside each slit, there is a nipple, and taking one of these in its mouth, the little beluga feels a surge of rich, warm milk flowing into its empty stomach. In the twenty months that follow, the young whale remains close to its mother and learns to converse in a number of low trilling notes, clicks, growls, short barks, and a series of birdlike sounds so varied and musical that white whales were once called "sea canaries."

When first born, an infant is grayish brown or a dark slate color with a possible misting of small spots. After many months have passed, its body gradually assumes a mottled appearance, becoming a pale slate gray, which eventually changes, when the young whale is half grown, to grayish yellow and then slowly fades, around six to seven years of age, to the light ivory or pure white of an adult. Its life normally spans twenty-five years, but this may extend to five decades.

Circumpolar in distribution, these delightful whales are a boreal species, found in high latitudes of the Arctic and adjacent areas with southern boundaries established at 49° north latitude in North America and 50° north latitude in eastern Asia. Geographically isolated populations are found in Lancaster Sound, Beaufort Sea, western Hudson Bay, Mackenzie River Delta, the St. Lawrence River, and near western Greenland. It is possible other populations in the Barents, White and Kara seas and the Bering and Beaufort seas also may prove to be isolated geographically.

White whales are found in the coastal waters of the arctic and subarctic regions.

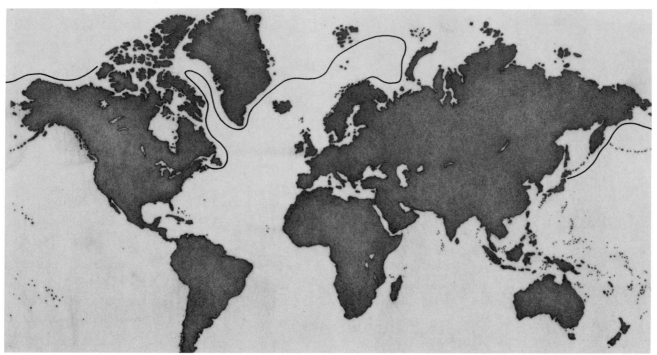

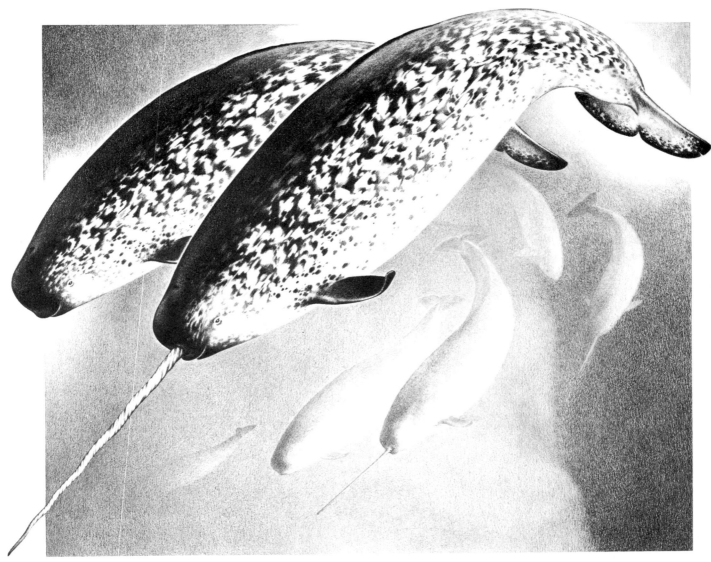

Narwhals exploring the pack ice.

Narwhal

Monodon monoceros

The name ''narwhal'' comes from the Norsemen of ancient Scandinavia and refers to a strange pattern of mottled streaks and spots that covers the smooth gray-white skin of *Monodon monoceros*. During the Middle Ages, when trade was established with southern lands, these shrewd Norsemen brought a treasure into the courts of medieval Europe, a splendid ivory shaft of great length and beauty, prized by kings and emperors as the horn of the legendary unicorn—an object of veneration that was, in fact, a single massive tooth taken from the head of a male narwhal.

In adult female whales, the two teeth in the upper jaw remain buried in the gums and seldom become visible. The great tusk of a male narwhal, however, erupts from the bony structure of its upper left jaw, pierces the upper lip, and grows straight outward in a counterclockwise spiral that may extend 8 to 9 feet (2.5 to 2.8 meters). The entire length of the tooth is incised with a deep, intricate grooving. Before birth, two teeth form in each side of the upper jaw of a fetus, but the back teeth do not develop and eventually are absorbed into the gums. In young males (and a few females), the left front tooth continues to grow until it extends into the famous long tusk, while the right front tooth usually remains small. On rare occasions, this second tooth may also grow into a thin spiral shaft.

The true function of the formidable left tusk has given rise to endless theories. Some describe it as an ice breaker or a probe for the ocean floor, while others maintain that the long tooth is a weapon used in combat by males for possession of females. Discarding theory, a careful examination of this impressive shaft reveals it to be hollow and somewhat fragile, with a core of soft, spongy tissue, rich in blood and exceedingly painful when injured. Many believe the tooth is a part of the body so specialized by evolution that it no longer is useful and now is limited to aggressive male display.

Excluding the tusk and measuring from nose to tail flukes, a narwhal reaches a length of 11 to 16 feet (3.5 to 5 meters) and a weight of 2,000 to 3,500 pounds (900 to 1,600 kilograms). Its head is relatively small and round, with no extension of a beak; the flippers have a semicurled tip, and the flukes are fan-shaped. Instead of a dorsal fin, there is a low ridge extending a short distance midway along its broad back. Newborn whales are slate gray; as they mature, this uniform color gradually changes to a pale brownish gray or ivory white with a marbling of irregular dark gray spots that forms a uniquely beautiful pattern on the upper part of the body. When they grow old, however, these spots may eventually fade to a shadowy cream-white.

In summer, sociable groups of six to ten whales gather in deepwater areas to descend as far as 1,000 feet (300 meters) into a twilight world of blue-black waters far beneath emerald-tinted icebergs to pursue turbot, skate,

Skull and left tooth of a male narwhal (ventral view).

Narwhal mother and infant.

arctic cod, sea scorpion, shrimp, and crab. There is a marked perference for squid, along with young halibut and silt-covered flounder.

As summer wanes and ice begins to film the water, most of the groups feeding in polar areas gather in large schools and migrate southward. Those that linger too long in departing are sometimes trapped, like the white whales, by a deepening ice barrier in the entrance of bays and fjords, confining them to a slowly shrinking enclosure where the whales, desperate for air, crowd around small breathing holes until they finally weaken and die. Most of the migrating groups avoid this danger and make their way to areas free of solid ice, where they pass the bleak months of winter in open water. By April, courtship among the narwhals is well underway, with small groups of males following unclaimed females. Those whales that remain apart from the amorous play are females approaching the end of fifteen months of gestation.

Early in June, when the pack ice begins to break up and drift apart, narwhals return to the Arctic Ocean, at times hiding in narrow leads, or cracks between splitting blocks of ice, to avoid killer whales patrolling the open water. A few newborn calves accompany their mothers on the northward journey, but most of the females make their way into familiar bays to await the time of birth. The little whales, born into frigid, ice-filled waters in mid-July, are wrapped in a warm, deep layer of blubber. They are 5 feet (1.5 meters) long, dark slate gray in color, and lack the mottled spotting of adults. Almost twenty months will pass before the young whales leave their mothers.

Narwhals prefer the chill, dark waters of the polar region extending along the coasts of North America, Greenland, Norway, and Russia. Their lives are passed in the splendid, savage land of the high Arctic, where the starry, still twilight of a northern summer night is lit by a midnight sun, where polar bears roam the rocky coastline and heavy fog lingers in the sheltering bays that provide a haven for these beautiful whales.

Range of narwhals in the Arctic Ocean.

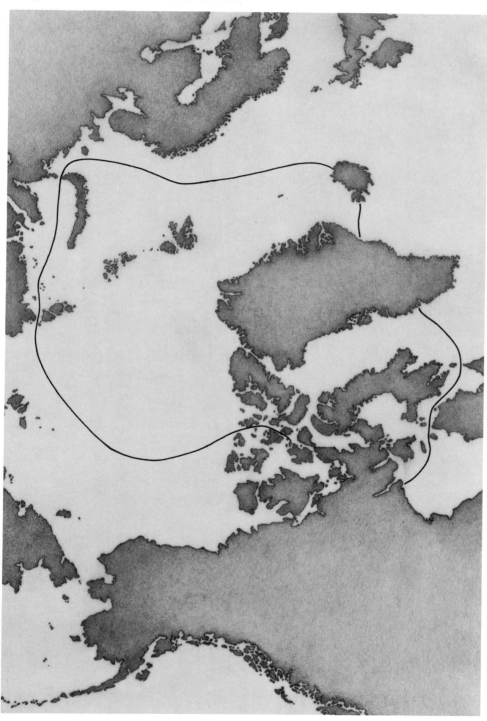

Dolphins: from top, rough-toothed dolphin, Atlantic hump-backed dolphin, and tucuxi.

Dolphins, Delphinidae

The family of true dolphins, Delphinidae, contains approximately seventeen genera and a very large number of species that are distinguished in a general way by certain structural characteristics. This deliberate vagueness is necessary because the many types of dolphins vary widely among themselves or resemble each other so closely as to cause confusion. Structurally, they have only four or five pairs of double-headed ribs, compared to the river dolphins' eight pairs; some of their neck vertebrae are fused; and their skulls lack the prominent crests that develop in beaked whales and sperm whales.

Apart from these distinctive features, dolphins are varied in size, ranging in length from the small tucuxi, measuring 3.6 feet (1.1 meters), up to the formidable killer whale, with a maximum length of 30.8 feet (9.4 meters). A few dolphins are stout instead of slender; some have a blunt or rounded snout instead of a beak; and almost all have teeth that are sharp, conical in shape, and numerous in both upper and lower jaws. Flippers may be pointed or paddle-like, and the dorsal fin may be triangular, falcate, or rounded, either rising high above the back or entirely absent.

Listed below are the first three members of this diverse family, followed by their common names, classifications, and numbers of species. The remaining fourteen genera of dolphins are listed in four similar sections that follow this introduction.

ROUGH-TOOTHED DOLPHIN
OTHER COMMON NAMES: rough-toothed porpoise, goggle-eyed porpoise
GENUS: *Steno*
SPECIES: rough-toothed dolphin, *Steno bredanensis,* the single species

ATLANTIC HUMP-BACKED DOLPHIN
OTHER COMMON NAME: West African many-toothed dolphin
GENUS: *Sousa*
SPECIES: There are two species in the genus *Sousa:*
    Atlantic hump-backed dolphin, *Sousa teuszii*
    Indo-Pacific hump-backed dolphin, *Sousa chinensis*

TUCUXI
OTHER COMMON NAMES: river dolphin, little bay dolphin
GENUS: *Sotalia*
SPECIES: tucuxi, *Sotalia fluviatilis,* the single species

Rough-toothed dolphins and small shark.

Rough-toothed Dolphin
Steno bredanensis

Rising out of blue-green depths, the long beak and lean form of the rough-toothed dolphin, *Steno bredanensis,* has the appearance of an ancient ichthyosaur, a group of fish-lizards that thrived in the warm waters of Mesozoic seas, millions of years ago. One of these extinct fish-lizards, *Stenopterygius,* was plump, smooth-skinned, and large-eyed, with lungs for breathing and a long beak lined with teeth. The modern *Steno bredanensis* is very similar in form to ancient *Stenopterygius,* with large, expressive brown eyes and a snout that is reptilian in outline, curving upward without break past the blowhole. Marked by a distinctive white lip line, the beak is compressed, with 20 to 27 remarkable teeth lining each side of both jaws. Instead of having smooth crowns, like other dolphins, the teeth of *Steno* are relatively large and extensively furrowed on top by fine vertical ridges.

Thin and sinewy, its strong body is characterized by a barrel chest, long dexterous flippers, and wide flukes that spread out from a slender caudal section. Body length is approximately 6.5 to 9 feet (2 to 2.7 meters). Among these dolphins, the dark, grayish skin on the back of a male is often marked with white streaks and erratic parallel lines which correspond in spacing to the strong, white teeth of a rival male. Surprisingly, a female may carry similar scars. The back is dark gray or violet black, fading to pale gray or white on the underside. Scattered in a random pattern over part of the body are white, pinkish-white, or ivory spots. These pale marks appear to be slightly raised areas of healed scar tissue that once may have been open wounds. The marks are more prevalent among dolphins in the open sea and those that dive deep when foraging. This painful mutilation is now known to occur from the bite of a small shark around 18 inches (45 centimeters) in length, equipped with a luminous body and projecting sawlike teeth capable of ripping a round chunk of flesh from the side of an unwary dolphin. This little squaloid, *Isistius brasiliensis,* is aptly called the "cookie-cutter shark."

While little information is available on the feeding habits of these dolphins, they are known to assemble in small groups containing a few members, possibly a family, or larger gatherings of up to fifty individuals, to patrol the edges of broad continental shelves rich in a variety of marine life. Judging from the preferences of captive dolphins, they consume small squid or schooling fish, and there is a report from Florida noting the presence of deepwater octopus in the stomach of a stranded specimen.

Rough-toothed dolphins sometimes accompany herds of bottlenose or spinner dolphins and schools of large tuna. They wander along the rim of the continental slope in temperate and deep tropical waters throughout the world, with small groups observed near the Hawaiian Islands and in the Mediterranean. Larger groups of the dolphins are found in the Pacific, Indian, and Atlantic oceans; they also occur in the Caribbean, the Red Sea, and the Bay of Bengal.

Cookie-cutter shark, *Isistius brasiliensis.*

Range of rough-toothed dolphins.

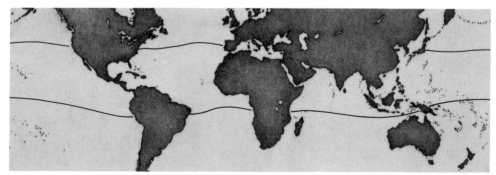

Dolphins pursuing mullet in coastal waters.

Atlantic Hump-backed Dolphin
Sousa teuszii

In past decades, the Atlantic hump-backed dolphin, *Sousa teuszii,* was considered to be very rare. This belief persisted until 1958 and 1959, when a number of these dolphins were observed at low tide, from January to April, swimming in the estuary of Douala, Cameroon, and in the rivers of Senegal, West Africa. Similar in shape and appearance to the bottlenose dolphin and the rough-toothed dolphin, they differed in the number of teeth, with a count of 23 to 31 on each side of both jaws. Length ranged up to approximately 9 feet (2.8 meters), and one dolphin weighed around 680 pounds (280 kilograms). Records of color vary, but the upper body is usually described as dark gray, sometimes fading to a lighter shade below. In *Sousa,* the dorsal fin is mounted on a prominent hump or ridge with a moderately low dorsal keel continuing down to the flukes, and a well-developed ventral keel appearing on the tail stock. Sometimes called the West African many-toothed dolphin, *S. teuszii* wanders along coastlines in groups of up to five individuals, searching for migrating schools of mullet, a favorite food item. Now reported along the Senegalese coast and the coast of Mauritania, it is reasonable to assume the range of the Atlantic hump-backed dolphin extends along the West African coast from Angola in the south to Mauritania in the north.

The Indo-Pacific hump-backed dolphin, or Chinese white dolphin, *Sousa chinensis,* is very beautiful. The body of this second species is pale ivory or pure white with a tint of pink on the underside; flippers, flukes, and dorsal fin are light gray-brown tinged with coral, and the eyes are brilliant black. Length is around 10 feet (3 meters), and the dental count of one specimen was 37 pairs of teeth in the upper jaw and 33 to 34 pairs in the lower jaw. These lovely dolphins occur from the Cape of Good Hope eastward through Indian, Indonesian, and Australian waters, particularly along the northeastern coastline, then up along the Indo-Chinese coast to the Canton River.

Indo-Pacific hump-backed dolphin.

Atlantic hump-backed dolphins occur along the western coast of Africa. Indo-Pacific hump-backed dolphins are found in the Indian and Pacific oceans.

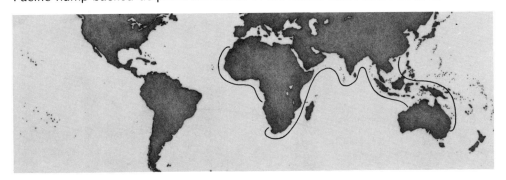

Little bay dolphins leaping high.

Tucuxi
Sotalia fluviatilis

Tucuxi, *Sotalia fluviatilis,* sometimes called the little bay dolphin, resembles a very small and dainty bottlenose dolphin. Its total length, of only 3.6 to 5.5 feet (1.1 to 1.7 meters) and weight of around 70 to 100 pounds (32 to 45 kilograms) have placed it in a special category, for tucuxi is considered to be the smallest member of Cetacea. Short and plump, it has a semifalcate dorsal fin, broad flippers, and flukes that are wide with a definite median notch. Its beak, shaped like a bottlenose dolphin's, has 26 to 35 teeth lining each side of the upper and lower jaws. In young dolphins, these teeth are sharp and well formed; as the dolphins age, however, abrasion from biting on the hard shells of crabs and prawns results in worn teeth. Adults have the pearl-gray tints and darker shades of a bottlenose dolphin but are often individually varied according to age and area. Generally, the back is a steel gray or brownish charcoal gray which extends to the flukes and flippers but fades to ivory or yellowish cream on the underside. This same pale shade sweeps upward toward the dorsal fin in two bands.

Bay dolphins are gregarious, usually traveling in small groups that glide, roll, and dive with effortless rhythm, maneuvering in close formation and leaping high above the surface. These excursions occur early in the morning and again in late afternoon, when they gather to hunt for prawns, crabs, or catfish hiding among tumbled rocks and matted water plants, and pursue schools of small fish that thrive in the braiding flow. Often accompanied by large Amazon dolphins, small tucuxi busily probe the brown waters of the great Amazon River as its slow currents move through the lush forests and savannahs of Brazil. They venture into the quiet flow of tributaries emptying into the river, some so heavily charged with decaying vegetation that the water is dark with residue. It is in this vast network of waterways, in the Amazon and Tocantins rivers and in the shallow coastal waters of northern South America, that the little bay dolphin makes its home.

The following dolphins, formerly considered as separate species, are now listed under the single species *Sotalia fluviatilis,* commonly called tucuxi.

The Guianan river dolphin, *Sotalia guianensis,* is found in the rivers and coastal waters of Guiana. It has a long beak, broad flippers, and a large dorsal fin; teeth number 35 to 36 on each side of both jaws and maximum length is around 5.5 feet (1.7 meters). In color, the back is dull brownish or leaden black, changing to a pale gray below, tinted with pink or a delicate violet.

The white dolphin, *Sotalia pallida,* is called "bufo blanco" by the natives of the Northern Amazon Basin. Its beak is short and thick; the dorsal fin is large, flippers are curved with a pointed tip, and body color is pale grayish ivory above and yellowish cream to ivory below.

The Brazilian dolphin, *Sotalia brasiliensis,* is found around the bay of Rio de Janeiro and the vast system of the Amazon River. Color varies from pale grayish blue to dark brown above, shading to a soft yellow on the sides and white on the underside.

Catfish.

The tucuxi is found in the Amazon and Tocantins rivers.

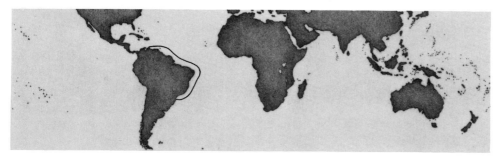

Dolphins: from top, striped dolphin, common dolphin, Risso's dolphin, and bottlenose dolphin.

Dolphins, Delphinidae (continued)

STRIPED DOLPHIN
OTHER COMMON NAMES: euphrosyne dolphin, blue-white dolphin, striped porpoise, ocean dolphin, streaker dolphin, Meyen's dolphin
GENUS: *Stenella*
SPECIES: The genus *Stenella* includes five species (present estimate):
Striped dolphin, *Stenella coeruleoalba*
Atlantic spotted dolphin, *Stenella plagiodon*
Spotted dolphin, *Stenella attenuata*
Clymene dolphin, *Stenella clymene*
Spinner dolphin, *Stenella longirostris*

COMMON DOLPHIN
OTHER COMMON NAMES: saddleback dolphin, white-bellied porpoise, crisscross dolphin
GENUS: *Delphinus*
SPECIES: common dolphin, *Delphinus delphis,* the single species

RISSO'S DOLPHIN
OTHER COMMON NAMES: gray grampus, white-headed grampus, mottled grampus
GENUS: *Grampus*
SPECIES: Risso's dolphin, *Grampus griseus,* the single species

BOTTLENOSE DOLPHIN
OTHER COMMON NAMES: bottlenose porpoise, gray porpoise
GENUS: *Tursiops*
SPECIES: bottlenose dolphin, *Tursiops truncatus,* the single species

Striped dolphins playing with a strand of seaweed.

Striped Dolphin
Stenella coeruleoalba

Trim and beautiful, the striped dolphin, *Stenella coeruleoalba,* is an appealing
blend of curiosity and playfulness. In search of entertainment, a group will
spend hours near the surface, teasing a flock of gulls or herding a school of
confused little fish through an obstacle course among the coral reefs. When a
long stem of kelp is discovered floating on the surface, competition flares and

the dolphins try to snatch the limber stalk from one another until an older dolphin finally surrenders the battered piece of seaweed to a pair of pleading young dolphins and watches them race away, pulling the pliable stem and whirling the slender brown blades into intricate patterns of flowing curves.

The striped dolphin is swift, its body strong and compact, with the sleek lines of a deepwater mammal. Its dorsal fin, high and falcate, is situated midway along the back; the flippers are small and sharply pointed, while the caudal section, heavily muscled and built for speed, tapers down to small flukes. The average length at maturity is around 6.8 feet (2.1 meters), and the maximum length is recorded at 9 feet (2.7 meters), with weight ranging up to 250 pounds (115 kilograms). The dolphin's back is dark indigo blue or blue-black in color, divided in midsection by a long, semi-white stripe. The flippers, flukes, and dorsal fin are pale gray to black; the sides are gray; and the underside, from lower jaw to abdomen, is a dazzling white. Both upper and lower jaws are edged with blue-black, and a black band spans the forehead, encircles the eye, and divides into one short line and a second, much longer line which continues down across the side to end on the ventral surface, with a third black stripe extending from the flipper past the eye. Inside the trim beak, there are 43 to 50 small teeth lining each side of the upper and lower jaws. These sharp little teeth are heavily enameled, with inward-curving tips that easily grasp and hold slippery scaled fish and fast-moving squid.

In temperate and semitropical waters, groups of hungry dolphins plunge deep to search for migrating schools of small fish by day and more exotic fare by night. When hunting in waters that vary in depth from 600 to well past 6,000 feet (100 to 1,000 fathoms), their feeding strategy is altered. As the sun sinks low on the horizon, striped dolphins carefully position themselves directly above underwater cliffs which loom over deep canyons, and, poised expectantly, they wait for dusk. Far down in the waters below, rising slowly out of the black obscurity of profound depths, drifting upward layer by layer as darkness falls, are strange creatures of the deep: the glistening forms of small lantern fish, their sides emblazoned with glowing blue photophores; hordes of diaphanous squids embroidered with a filigree of shimmering points of light; and bright-eyed shrimps of brilliant crimson hues. Diving down to meet these fairylike creatures, the dolphins sometimes descend 650 feet (200 meters) into a deepening gloom to pursue phantom forms of azure, emerald, crimson, and gold that lace the darkness of the lower depths with jeweled splendor.

As darkness falls, shrimp, squid, and small lantern fish rise toward the surface.

As the nocturnal feast ends and dawn approaches, the school begins to circle slowly, gathering into a closely packed mass that constantly surfaces to breathe and sinks back to drowse in a rest period of three to five hours. On the outer fringe of the quiet assembly, a few members may remain alert and watchful. They are wary for good reason, because striped dolphins are subject to attack from several enemies; flukes and flippers are occasionally torn, and some individuals carry ugly scars across their backs or caudal areas, deep circular wounds that only the jaws of a great shark could inflict. Even more deadly are roving packs of killer whales that prey on migrating schools of

An infant dolphin remains very close to its mother.

dolphins traveling northward in May through June in the North Pacific above 30° north latitude and returning to the south in September through December.

It is possible that striped dolphins have two separate breeding seasons, since births occur in spring and again in autumn. Born into the warm waters of subtropical areas, the small gray-and-white calf, approximately 3 feet (1 meter) in length, swims close to its mother's side, at times resting its little flukes on those of the mother to be propelled along by her strong thrust. When six to nine months of age, it is given more freedom to mingle with the group and allowed to roam with its playmates. At around two years of age, it joins other young dolphins to form large schools that are loosely attached to the family units. Then, at a certain time and without warning, these schools of immature young dolphins leave the adults and venture out into the open sea. They are playful and prone to frolic, but are extremely wary of any strange object, and, acting as a closely knit group, they gather strength, skill, and knowledge in testing the sea. Roaming the vast ocean until they reach maturity at six years of age, the wandering dolphins individually enter adult groups. Their life span is estimated to be twenty-five to fifty years. First recorded from the Río de la Plata, between Argentina and Uruguay, striped dolphins occur in the North Atlantic from Nova Scotia south to Jamaica and the Gulf of Mexico; other areas include the temperate waters of the Mediterranean, the continental slopes, and the warm Gulf Stream. Isolated populations have been recorded near Durban, South Africa, and in the Pacific Ocean, suggesting a pattern of local populations worldwide.

The genus *Stenella* contains several species: two are well defined, while the remainder are of uncertain status and require extensive examination in order to identify valid species. At this time, both the striped dolphin, *Stenella coeruleoalba,* and the spinner dolphin, *Stenella longirostris,* are well established. Apart from these two species, the category of spotted dolphins has been filled with a number of nominal types. Among the established names listed are the Atlantic spotted dolphin, *S. plagiodon;* the spotted dolphin, *S. attenuata;* and the clymene dolphin, *S. clymene.* Those of doubtful status include *S. capensis,* discovered to be synonymous with *S. attenuata;* the spotted dolphin, *S. graffmani,* now known to be a geographical variant of *S. attenuata;* and the bridled dolphin, *S. frontalis,* now considered to be a subspecies of *S. clymene.*

Range of striped dolphins in temperate and tropical waters.

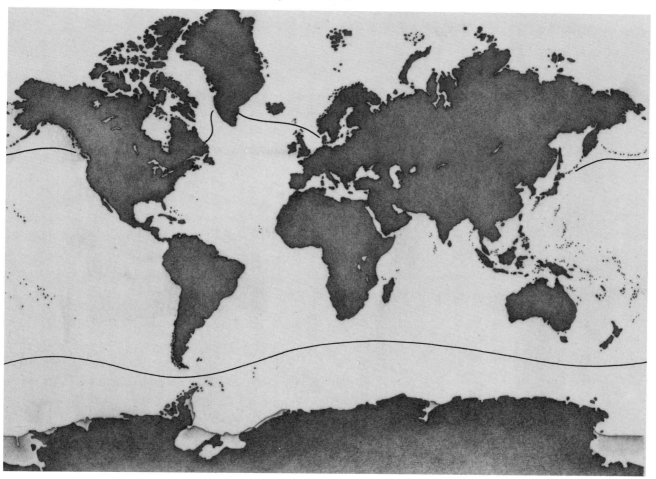

SPECIES OF *STENELLA*

Striped Dolphin, *Stenella coeruleoalba* **(A).** The striped dolphin has a maximum length of 9 feet (2.7 meters) and resembles the common dolphin. Its beak is long and narrow, with 43 to 50 pairs of teeth in the upper and lower jaws. In color, the back is deep indigo blue, fading to pure white on the abdomen. Striped dolphins occur in the Atlantic and Pacific oceans and the Mediterranean Sea.

Atlantic Spotted Dolphin, *Stenella plagiodon* **(B, C, D).** The Atlantic spotted dolphin reaches a maximum length of 8 feet (2.4 meters) and has a tooth count of 28 to 35 in each side of the upper jaw and 30 to 36 in each side of the lower jaw. From birth to maturity, there is a continuing change in color patterns. Born without spots, an infant dolphin (B) has a violet-gray back fading to pure white on the underside. As it grows, a scattering of light spots appears on its lower side, then gradually spreads upward onto the back, while a dark spotting begins to appear on the white skin of its belly (C). The development of this characteristic spotting pattern progresses until all demarcation lines are obliterated and the entire body becomes dark, overspread with small, pale spots (D), leaving unmarked only a white lip line, the dorsal fin, flippers, flukes, and a partially obliterated spinal blaze. Sometimes called the long-snouted dolphin, Gulf Stream spotted dolphin, spotter, or spotted porpoise, these dolphins may assemble in hundreds, but more often gather in small groups to search for squid or pursue herring, anchovies, jacks, and immature eels in the North Atlantic from 39° north latitude southward to Venezuela.

Spotted Dolphin, *Stenella attenuata* **(E).** Slender and streamlined, the spotted dolphin has a low, extended forehead, a high, falcate dorsal fin, and small flippers that are placed far forward on the sides. Its back is dark bluish gray fading to grayish white on the belly, with small white, purple, or gray spots scattered over the body. Except for a distinctive white tip, the long, narrow beak is black with a black line extending to encircle the eye. A tooth count of one specimen listed 41 to 45 in each side of the upper jaw and 40 to 43 in each side of the lower jaw. Body length ranges from 5.2 to 7.8 feet (1.6 to 2.4 meters), and weight is listed at approximately 176 pounds (80 kilograms) for deep-ocean dolphins, while larger coastal dolphins register a hefty 280 pounds (127 kilograms).

Spotted dolphins feed on fish and squid found in the middle and upper levels. Both of these, especially the gauze-winged flying fish, are also hunted by schools of large, voracious tuna that gather beneath a group of dolphins and persist in following them, perhaps using the dolphins as a food-finding mechanism. Shy and graceful, *S. attenuata* is usually found far from shore in tropical and subtropical waters of the Atlantic and Pacific oceans. Two additional types, *S. graffmani* and *S. capensis,* are nominal variations of the spotted dolphin, *Stenella attenuata.*

Species of *Stenella:* from top, striped dolphin, *S. coeruleoalba;* Atlantic spotted dolphin, *S. plagiodon,* infant, juvenile, and adult; spotted dolphin, *S. attenuata.*

SPECIES OF *STENELLA*

Clymene Dolphin, *Stenella clymene.* Closely related to the spinner dolphin, the clymene dolphin has a dark gray dorsal cape that changes abruptly to a pale gray band on the sides, then fades to a white ventral surface flecked with small dark spots. Flippers, flukes, and dorsal fin are blackish gray in color. *S. clymene* differs from *S. longirostris* in having a broad, curving dip in the dorsal cape, a converging dark stripe leading from flipper to eye, a whitish blaze (or streak) from blowhole to forehead crease, and a black-tipped beak bordered by grayish-white extensions of the ventral white. In *S. clymene,* the beak is shorter, the flippers and dorsal fin somewhat smaller, and the body form more robust than *S. longirostris.* Length ranges between 5.5 to 7 feet (1.7 to 2.1 meters), and its small sharp teeth number 38 to 49 in each side of the upper jaw and 38 to 47 in each side of the lower jaw.

Clymene dolphins appear to prefer depths ranging from 820 to 16,400 feet (250 to 5,000 meters), where, long after sundown, they search for small squid and fish, including lantern fish. Their range is limited to the warm waters of the tropical and subtropical Atlantic with no record of occurrence in the Indian or Pacific oceans.

Named *Stenella clymene* by Hershkovitz in 1966, the clymene dolphin was introduced as a valid species in August of 1981 when W. F. Perrin, E. D. Mitchell, J. G. Mead, D. K. Caldwell, and P. J. H. van Bree published the results of their studies of *S. clymene* in the *Journal of Mammalogy,* Vol. 62, no. 3, under the title "STENELLA CLYMENE, A Rediscovered Tropical Dolphin Of The Atlantic."

Spinner Dolphin, *Stenella longirostris.* These dolphins are famed for a series of spinning performances that begin with a dazzling rotation of the dolphin's body, whirling on its longitudinal axis. The most spectacular display, however, is a great soaring arc upward and forward; then, at the top of this arc, the dolphin cartwheels, tail over head, leaving a sweep of glittering spray before slipping back into the sea tail first.

Slender in form and sylphlike, adult dolphins range in length from 5.5 feet (1.65 meters) to 7 feet (2.1 meters). Both flippers and flukes are narrow and pointed, but the shape of the dorsal fin in male dolphins varies according to geographic region, being triangular (Costa Rican and whitebelly types), slightly falcate (Hawaiian type), or canted forward (eastern type). All but the Hawaiian dolphins are marked by a postanal bulge on the lower tail stock. The beak of *S. longirostris* is unusually long and contains more teeth than any other dolphin, with 47 to 64 pairs of teeth in the upper and lower jaws. The back is dark gray, the sides are gray, and the underside is pale gray or white often flecked with very small spots. Found in the Atlantic, Pacific, and Indian oceans, spinner dolphins can be identified by a black lip line and a beak that is dark on top and light below with a black tip.

Species of *Stenella:* clymene dolphin. *S. clymene;* spinner dolphin, *S. longirostris.*

These charming little sprites streak away at 25 knots when chasing flying fish.

Common Dolphin
Delphinus delphis

Small, swift and graceful, the common dolphin, *Delphinus delphis,* often travels with a noisy group of companions that leap high above the sunlit surface in a scalloping of sleek forms, proceeding at an easy pace of 5 to 7 miles per hour (4 to 6 knots). When pursuing squid or flying fish, however, these charming little sprites are capable of streaking away at a speed of 29 miles per hour (25 knots).

Delphinus, one of the smallest dolphins, has an overall length that varies from 5 feet (1.5 meters) up to a maximum 8.5 feet (2.6 meters) and a weight that ranges up to 300 pounds (136 kilograms). Males are found to be slightly larger than females. Common dolphins resemble striped dolphins *(Stenella* species) in outward appearance: the dorsal fin may be either falcate with a pointed tip or almost triangular in form; flippers and flukes are small; and the beak, sharply divided from the lower forehead by a deep groove, is narrow and tapered, with 40 to 50 sharp teeth lining each side of the upper and lower jaws. Color varies widely and can best be described as black or dark brown on the back and white or cream-white on the belly, with a dark line stretching from flipper to lower jaw. Both flippers and flukes are dark and the eyes are circled by black areas that extend to the beak. An examination of the coloring of *D. delphis* reveals a strong pattern of two oblique lines crossing to form an X on the dolphin's side, dividing its color into black above and white below, with a band of buffy tan in front and a band of gray in back. The shape of this crisscross pattern is distinctive and has bestowed on this small cetacean the descriptive name of crisscross dolphin.

The name "dolphin" has been applied to two completely dissimilar marine animals. The first one is the familiar common dolphin, a warm-blooded mammal of legendary fame. The second one is the dorado, *Coryphaena hippurus,* a long-finned pelagic fish of spectacular color and speed.

Common dolphins seldom travel alone, preferring to gather in small groups of up to twenty individuals or assemble in large numbers to follow shoals of squid or schools of young herring, pilchard, and anchovy, along with nocturnal hake. Like striped dolphins, they usually feed at approximately the same time during the night or day. When they overtake a large school of anchovies, each dolphin rushes into the center of the mass to seize as many fish as possible and swallow them whole.

These feeding forays are often joined by bands of bottlenose or white-sided dolphins and a number of shy right whale dolphins, alternately chasing

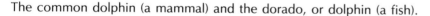

The common dolphin (a mammal) and the dorado, or dolphin (a fish).

Common dolphins diving for cephalopods.

and feeding on the small fish or squid. Their foraging lasts around one hour, then the groups reassemble and return to other activities and play patterns. If schools of fish become scarce and food is difficult to find, these large gatherings of dolphins break up into small groups which wander away in all directions. In higher latitudes, when the first storms of late autumn move over white-capped water, females and their young often assemble in large companies to face the rigors of winter, depending on their extended numbers to find food and on their speed and caution for protection. It is thought that male dolphins live apart from the large herds, maintaining a considerable distance from the females but remaining in the same general area until the rough winds and churning seas give way to the warmth of spring.

Among common dolphins, courtship occurs in the spring and fall, followed within ten or eleven months by the birth of infant dolphins measuring approximately 30 to 34 inches (75 to 86 centimeters). The newborn immediately become part of a family group composed of three to five females accompanied by their young, led and guarded by a male dolphin. The mothers often share the responsibility of caring for little dolphins by taking turns in watching over the active youngsters. The life span of *D. delphis* is estimated to be more than twenty-five years.

Widely distributed in temperate and tropical seas, common dolphins are found throughout the Atlantic and Pacific oceans, at times following the Gulf Stream up to Norwegian waters, but seldom venturing into the Arctic. They are abundant in the Mediterranean Sea around Gibraltar and in the Black Sea. Scattered populations are found in the Indian Ocean and the waters near Japan.

There has been such extensive regional variation of body color and length of beak in *D. delphis* that a large number of species has been listed in past decades. These included Baird's dolphin, cape dolphin, red-bellied dolphin and a variety of other geographical divisions. At this time, however, all of these are considered to be variants of the single species *Delphinus delphis.*

One subspecies of the common dolphin, called the Pacific dolphin, or

Baird's dolphin, *Delphinus bairdii,* is found in the North Pacific from British Columbia, Canada, southward to Mexico. It is a stouter form of the common dolphin, with a length of approximately 7 feet (2.2 meters), a narrow beak, and broad-based flippers. While similar in form and general color to *D. delphis,* there are some slight differences: the distinctive yellow ocher bands are missing in *D. bairdii,* and the dark stripes, running from eye to anus and from lower jaw to base of flippers, are pale.

The cape dolphin, *Delphinus capensis,* is another form of the common dolphin, found near the Cape of Good Hope, with observations reported from Kyushu, Japan, and a possible distribution in the Atlantic and Indian oceans. It resembles the typical *D. delphis* in form and general color but has a longer beak. In this dolphin, change in the standard color pattern is limited to a single pale stripe instead of the two dark stripes stretching from eye to anus.

The third form of *D. delphis* is the red-bellied dolphin, *Delphinus roseiventris.* It is reported from the Torres Strait, between New Guinea and the northern tip of Australia, the Molucca Sea, east of the Celebes Islands, and the Banda Sea, north of the island of Timor in the Greater Sunda Islands. *D. roseiventris* is distinguished by a pale, rose-colored tint on its underside.

Range of common dolphins.

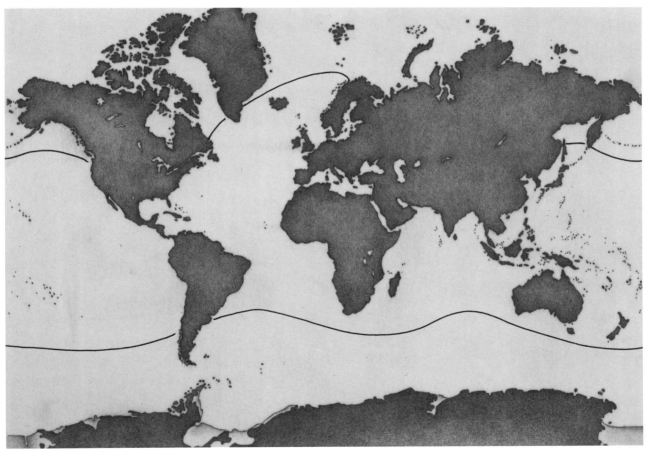

Pale and battle-scarred, an aged Risso's dolphin teases a frightened octopus.

Risso's Dolphin
Grampus griseus

Swift and powerful, Risso's dolphin, *Grampus griseus,* often forgets its customary caution when joined by other dolphins and becomes playful, showing an aptitude for wave-hopping, spectacular leaps, and sudden wild chases down into the depths, at times turning aside to chase a small shark into hiding or nip at a large octopus, which turns white with fright. Full of waggish humor, it sometimes rises out of the water and swims backward, head up, sitting on its tail, before rolling over and vanishing beneath the waves.

The name *Grampus* is derived from the French words *grand poisson*, meaning "big fish" or "fat fish." Risso's dolphin deserves this unflattering title because the front part of its body is unusually round and robust, while the back part, from a point slightly past the dorsal fin, narrows down to a slender tail stock. Overall body measurement is listed at 12 to 14 feet (3.6 to 4.3 meters). The dorsal fin, rising midway along its back, is very high and falcate; the flippers are remarkably long, and the flukes have a concave rear border with a deep center notch. Its head is round, with a blunt snout curving upward from the lip line, and on its forehead, along the body axis, there is an odd, V-shaped crease which divides the melon and is a definitive characteristic of *G. griseus*. Other dolphins have an impressive array of sharp teeth, but Risso's dolphin must manage with only 2 to 7 teeth on each side of the lower jaw, near the tip. In older adults, all of these teeth are worn down to the gum line or have dropped out, leaving the dolphin more or less toothless, a condition that usually causes little inconvenience, since this species, like the beaked whales, is limited to small squid as a principal food.

Wandering through temperate and tropical oceans in random groups or as solitary individuals, they advance into higher latitudes and colder waters during the summer months to probe the depths for small, fast squid and shy octopus. In search of such elusive quarry, they examine the broad continental shelves, exploring the swift flow of the Gulf Stream or deep waters of the Benguela Current, and even venture along such bleak shores as the coast of Chile and Peru. In this region, the coastline is formed by the lofty Andes Mountains, a range of towering peaks which descends gradually to a barren region near ocean level, then plunges downward in a precipitous drop-off to the profound depths of the Peru-Chile Trench, a descent of around 9 miles (15 kilometers).

When they enter these waters, the dolphins move through one of the richest feeding areas on earth, created by the wind and a great ocean current moving northward. In the South Pacific, the Humboldt Current rises where the tip of South America extends into the West Wind Drift to divide the Southern Ocean and divert part of its flow into a northern course. Moving like a vast river, several hundred miles wide, this mighty current flows along the western coast of Chile and Peru, surrounding the dolphins with noisy flocks of cormorants, pelicans, and boobies flying overhead while immense shoals of anchovies stream through the blue-green waters below. As the current surges past the barren coastline and the Andes Mountains, a strong south wind, blowing along the coast, continually pushes inshore layers of surface water outward, setting in motion a rolling movement that curves downward in a vast spiral to force the cold, dense layers of deep water welling upward to replace the outward-bound surface layers. This upwelling of mineral-laden water has made the Humboldt Current exceedingly rich in fertilizers, which provide nourishment for swarms of plankton and attract fish, squid, diving birds, seals, sea lions, and whales. In these teeming waters, Risso's dolphins feast on schools of small squid that gather near the surface under cover of darkness.

The dolphin sometimes swims backward.

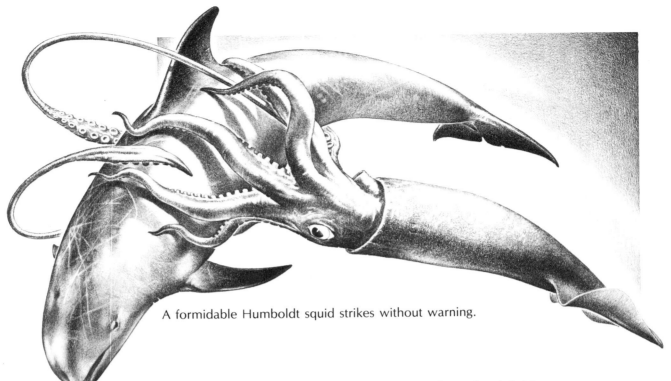

A formidable Humboldt squid strikes without warning.

As they journey along the Peruvian coastline, the dolphins may pass over an area where danger waits. In waters near Cabo Blanco, Peru, where the Humboldt Current curves westward, squid of the species *Ommastrephes gigas* patrol the lower levels by day, gliding through the murky gloom like phantom shadows. Although they lack the size of giant squid, usually reaching a length of 7 to 13 feet (2.2 to 4 meters)—a measurement equal to that of an adult grampus, their attack is swift, and the bite of their large, parrot-like beaks is formidable; so much so that many naturalists consider this species to be the most dangerous invertebrate living today. Like the primitive sharks, these squid are unpredictable; even a large one, when injured, is immediately wrapped in long tentacles and torn apart by its companions. Prowling deep submarine canyons by day, the squid drift upward after the sun has set and darkness spreads over the ocean. They appear as sudden streaks of movement when chasing small squid in the upper levels. At other times, they lie quiet, floating on the surface, their eyes glowing in the darkness. Passing through this region, Risso's dolphins carry scars that may have been made by these carnivorous creatures, long white streaks and deep pressure marks from circular suckers armed with claws, which bear silent witness to deadly battles fought far below the tranquil surface of a moonlit sea.

Little information is available on the breeding and birth of *Grampus griseus,* but an examination of a stranded female dolphin carrying a full-term fetus has established a probable time of birth around the end of the year. At birth, an infant dolphin is light gray; as it grows older, this neutral shade gradually changes to grayish black tinged with blue or purple, and the underside develops a large area of grayish-white splotches. In contrast, the dorsal fin, flippers, and flukes usually remain black. The dark back of an adult dolphin is streaked and spotted with a dense webbing of pale scars apparently made by the blunt teeth of aggressive rivals, or the tentacles and beaks of large squid.

As it grows old, however, the dark color of the torso eventually fades to a ghostly silver gray or cream white, with the head becoming almost entirely white.

Through the centuries, these dolphins have attracted a wide variety of common names, beginning with Risso's porpoise, gray grampus, mottled grampus, white blackfish, and white-headed grampus. Also, contrary to their cautious nature, some have become well known. One large dolphin in the Pacific has become a legend: Pelorus Jack was a Risso's dolphin that patrolled the shipping lanes between Wellington, Australia, and Nelson, New Zealand, playing near the bows of ships and leading them safely into the entrance of Pelorus Sound. This self-appointed pilot was given lifelong protection by an order-in-council from the government and faithfully continued to guide ships into safe harbor for twenty-four years, until it disappeared in 1912.

Worldwide in distribution, these quaint dolphins prefer the warm waters of temperate and tropical regions where the depth is greater than 600 feet (100 fathoms). They are found in the Atlantic Ocean from Newfoundland and Sweden down to the tip of South America and Cape Town, South Africa. Reports also list the Mediterranean Sea, the Indonesian Archipelago, and the Pacific Ocean from Japan down to Australia and Chile.

Range of Risso's dolphins.

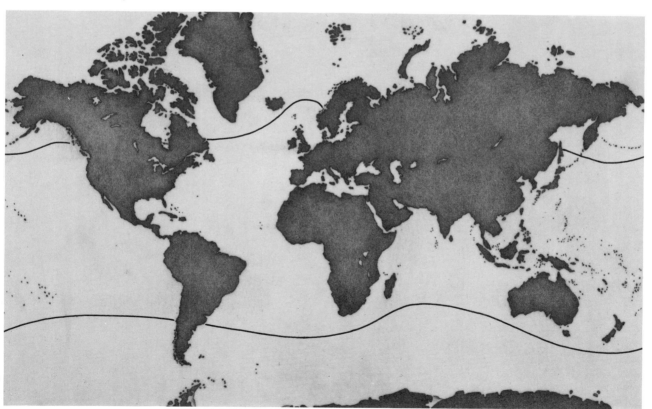

Male bottlenose dolphins attacking a large shark.

Bottlenose Dolphin
Tursiops truncatus

In areas where large sharks are numerous, the birth of a dolphin is accompanied by singular peril. To meet this emergency, bottlenose dolphins surround a mother and her newborn infant with a protective shield of adults, flanked by several large males that serve as guardians, tense and alert as they move out in advance of the group to scan the surrounding waters. Sometimes, far down on the ocean floor, there is a quickening of movement as a familiar drama begins to unfold. Reacting to the scent of birth blood, sharks begin to rise out of the depths, led by the shadowy form of a great white shark. When this ominous presence is located, the guardian males swing back to confront the advancing figure and gradually close in a large circle around it.

From the perimeter of the circle, a male dolphin surges in to strike the shark full force in its soft underbelly, rupturing the liver or intestines, while a second male rips into the gill covers of the great fish. Wounded in two vital areas, it whips around in agony, drifting lower in the dark blue water until surrounded by a pack of smaller sharks that converge in a whirling frenzy of tearing jaws and streaking forms. At this point, the dolphins quietly depart. Those who have witnessed such events attest not only to the dolphins' courage, but also to their intelligence and discipline.

Robust in body and moderate in size, bottlenose dolphins range in length from 9 feet (2.7 meters) to a maximum of 13 feet (4 meters) and weigh from 500 pounds (230 kilograms) to more than 1,440 pounds (650 kilograms), with males slightly larger than females. The dorsal fin is tall and falcate, situated midway on the back; flippers are broad, with a curved outer edge, and flukes are rather large. Marked by an extended lower jaw, the beak is relatively short and bottle-like in shape, with 18 to 26 teeth lining each side of the upper and lower jaws. As age advances, these sharp teeth gradually wear away until a very old dolphin is often left with hard, toothless gums.

Mother dolphin
and newborn infant.

Young dolphin and small shark.

There is a slight variation in color. The back is bluish gray or slate gray, with lighter gray sides and white or ivory pink on the underside from lower jaw to flukes. The head, flippers, and flukes are deep gray, with an occasional dark spotting appearing on the ventral surface of aged females. There are also subtle shadings, such as the "bridle stripe" around the eye and a second light stripe from the eye to the ear and down to the flipper, with a sharp demarcation between the white throat and the gray neck. A dorsal "cape," or dark shading, swings back from the beak, spreading over the top of the head and down along the sides to gradually fade behind the dorsal fin. It should be noted that some of the dolphins observed in the Gulf of California and in the waters around Central America are described as black on the back.

Bottlenose dolphins are gregarious and travel in groups of two to twelve individuals, or large assemblies of up to five hundred members with small groups accompanying great whales such as humpbacks, blue whales, or right whales. Larger dolphins are usually found in deep waters covering the outer edge of the continental shelf, but small dolphins ride the incoming tide to linger in sheltered bays and harbors. They explore large river channels and play in the pounding surf, at times leaping far above the surface, with some even spinning longitudinally on their body axis.

When hungry, the dolphins scythe through schools of small herring, swallowing them whole and head first, snapped up by a flick of their dexterous beaks. Inshore, they sweep the gullies and dark recesses for catfish, eels, and other bottom fishes, and off the coast of North America, they follow shoals of mullet and gizzard shad. Around coral reefs, they search the sand floors for hidden skates or rays and any small sharks that have failed to find cover. Lacking experience, there are times when younger dolphins give way to foolish impulse. One juvenile found stranded on a British beach had died of

The food of bottlenose dolphins includes shrimp, squid, herring, mullet, mackerel, catfish, eel, shark, skate, octopus, and cuttlefish.

strangulation, a condition brought on when the 6.5-foot (2-meter) dolphin swallowed a 4-foot (1.3-meter) shark. Unable to accommodate the lengthy meal, the dolphin expired with the shark's tail hanging from its beak.

A definite variation in size occurs in small dolphins, indicating a period of several months in which the young are born, or possibly marking two separate breeding seasons. In early spring or fall, the ritual of mating intensifies as the posturing of courting pairs gives way to a more passionate play when they swim side by side, sometimes touching, sometimes chasing each other with playful nips on flippers and flukes until union is accomplished.

After eleven or twelve months, as the time of birth approaches, a second female begins to accompany the expectant mother, remaining very close to her. The actual birth requires twenty minutes or more to deliver an infant 35 to 50 inches (90 to 130 centimeters) long and weighing 26 pounds (12 kilograms). Born directly into the water with limp flukes rolled and both flippers and dorsal fin folded to its body, the baby arrives tail first, its head appearing last, and instantly struggles toward the surface to draw its first, gasping breath. In her estimated thirty-five years of life, the female, maturing at age five to twelve, will give birth to approximately eight young.

A very young dolphin is kept close to its mother's side, well away from strange or dangerous objects, from fights between other dolphins, and out from under descending high jumpers that crash down through the surface. As the small dolphin grows, it may become so venturesome the mother must enforce discipline. One worried female swam above her mischievous young and pinned it to the floor, holding it there by force for thirty seconds. A second mother turned belly up on the surface and held her squirming young one in the air. When normal activities were resumed, the little dolphins were subdued and docile.

In the months that follow, the playful youngsters learn to chase small fish

Courtship of bottlenose dolphins.

Dolphins, Delphinidae (continued)

PACIFIC WHITE-SIDED DOLPHIN
OTHER COMMON NAME: Pacific white-striped dolphin
GENUS: *Lagenorhynchus*
SPECIES: The genus *Lagenorhynchus* includes six species:
Pacific white-sided dolphin, *Lagenorhynchus obliquidens*
Atlantic white-sided dolphin, *Lagenorhynchus acutus*
White-beaked dolphin, *Lagenorhynchus albirostris*
Dusky dolphin, *Lagenorhynchus obscurus*
Hourglass dolphin, *Lagenorhynchus cruciger*
Peale's dolphin, *Lagenorhynchus australis*

MELON-HEADED WHALE
OTHER COMMON NAMES: many-toothed blackfish, broad-headed dolphin,
broad-beaked dolphin, little killer whale, Hawaiian blackfish
GENUS: *Peponocephala*
SPECIES: melon-headed whale, *Peponocephala electra,* the single species

PYGMY KILLER WHALE
OTHER COMMON NAMES: slender blackfish, slender pilot whale
GENUS: *Feresa*
SPECIES: pygmy killer whale, *Feresa attenuata,* the single species

COMMERSON'S DOLPHIN
OTHER COMMON NAMES: piebald porpoise, *le jacobite*
GENUS: *Cephalorhynchus*
SPECIES: There are four species of the genus *Cephalorhynchus:*
Commerson's dolphin, *Cephalorhynchus commersonii*
Heaviside's dolphin, *Cephalorhynchus heavisidii*
Black dolphin, *Cephalorhynchus eutropia*
Hector's dolphin, *Cephalorhynchus hectori*

Pacific white-sided dolphins leap high in the early-morning light.

Pacific White-sided Dolphin
Lagenorhynchus obliquidens

Along the rugged coastline, as morning mist dissolves in the first rays of a rising sun, light gleams on the sleek heads of sea lions and tints the wispy vapor of their breath. Rising out of the mirrored water near them, a group of dolphins leap high above the surface, flinging themselves up in soaring arcs to crash down on their sides or bellies. In sheer exuberance, a few somersault forward, tail over head, to land in jets of flying spray.

The Pacific white-sided dolphin, *Lagenorhynchus obliquidens,* is small, measuring around 7 to 8 feet (2.1 to 2.4 meters) in length and ranging in weight from 300 to 330 pounds (135 to 150 kilograms). Compared to a bottlenose dolphin, its beak is very short, with 22 to 33 pairs of sharp teeth lining the upper and lower jaws, useful in nipping the toes of passing sea turtles. Its body is robust, tapering rapidly toward the flukes, with a large falcate dorsal fin rising in a high curve above the back. Placed forward on the body, its flippers have a curved leading edge and a semiround tip, while the flukes are narrow, tapered, and have a small median notch.

In this dolphin, a balanced design of color and form has produced an unusually beautiful effect. The upper body is jet black, changing to grayish white on the sides, with a wide, pale stripe curving forward across its black back. The ventral, or lower, surface is brilliant white, separated from pale gray sides by a black line that forms a very prominent border, curving from the mouth to the base of the flippers, then ending at the caudal section. The dorsal fin is black with a pale gray posterior edge, while the head and both upper and lower lips are black.

Aggressively sociable, white-sided dolphins actively seek company, joining shy right whale dolphins and, more rarely, striped dolphins. Groups of twenty-five to one hundred are common, but assemblies may increase to two thousand or more when white-sided dolphins combine with large groups of bottlenose or common dolphins to sweep through the depths in vigorous pursuit of squid or small pelagic fish.

These great assemblies gather in certain areas to feed on schools of northern anchovies. Vast shoals of this small fish range from Lower California up to the cold waters of British Columbia, following and feeding on floating concentrations of copepods and other plankton, only to be followed, in turn, by a horde of hungry dolphins. When schools of anchovies are not available, a different strategy is tried. After the sun has set and darkness closes over the water, groups of dolphins, using a broad sweep of sonar, dive deep to search the bottom for hake, a codlike fish that is active at night, feeding on crustaceans and other small marine animals.

Nipping at a passing sea turtle.

Pacific white-sided dolphin and Atlantic white-sided dolphin.

In autumn, the dolphins leave the open ocean and move inshore in a seasonal migration that is necessary to follow their food supply. As the winds increase in fall, great schools of herring leave their feeding grounds in deep water and move in flowing rivers of fish toward the shallow waters of familiar bays where the females lay their eggs, thirty thousand per female, attaching them to seaweed growing in warm, sunny inlets. Moving close behind the herring are white-sided dolphins, darting through the densely packed mass to feed until gorged, then withdrawing to trail the shimmering multitude.

Mating and birth occur from February to May, or September to November, when the dolphins migrate to the open sea or back to inshore waters. In spring or fall, approximately one year after the breeding period has passed, young dolphins measuring around 31 to 35 inches (80 to 90 centimeters) in length are born into cold northern waters.

Confined to the North Pacific Ocean, Pacific white-sided dolphins are found from Magdalena Bay, Baja California, up to Amchitka, Alaska, in the east. Those in the western Pacific are found in the Sea of Japan northward along the coast of Japan up to Kamchatka, U.S.S.R. At this time, the genus *Lagenorhynchus* contains five additional species: the Atlantic white-sided dolphin, white-beaked dolphin, dusky dolphin, hourglass dolphin, and Peale's dolphin. The status of the dusky dolphin has been questioned by many cetologists.

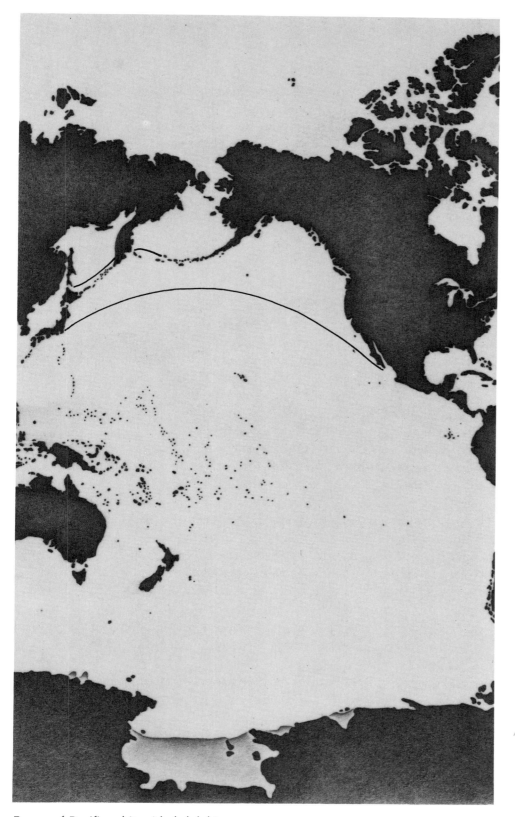

Range of Pacific white-sided dolphins.

SPECIES OF *LAGENORHYNCHUS*

Pacific White-sided Dolphin, *Lagenorhynchus obliquidens.* Limited to the North Pacific Ocean, these small dolphins measure around 7 to 8 feet (2.1 to 2.4 meters) in length. They are short-beaked with a high dorsal fin, hooked flippers, and 22 to 33 pairs of teeth in each side of the jaws. The back is black, the sides are gray, and the belly is white.

Atlantic White-sided Dolphin, *Lagenorhynchus acutus.* In this dolphin, the caudal section is surprisingly thick, extremely long, and strongly compressed laterally, with definite ridges on the dorsal and ventral surfaces which curve abruptly into the flukes. Color is arranged in a handsome pattern. The dolphin has a jet-black back and white belly, separated by conspicuous lateral bands of white and grayish or yellowish tan on its sides. Maximum length is around 9 feet (2.75 meters). The dorsal fin is tall, falcate, and either black or bicolor, while the beak, short and invariably black in color, has 30 to 40 teeth lining the two sides of each jaw.

Sometimes called "jumpers," Atlantic white-sided dolphins usually gather in groups of ten to fifty, but are known to assemble in herds of up to a thousand that roam the cold currents of the North Atlantic Ocean in the wake of squid and herring. Courtship is followed within eleven to twelve months, in late summer, by the birth of the young, measuring approximately 45 inches (115 centimeters) in length.

L. acutus is found in the cold waters of the Labrador Current from southern Greenland and the Davis Strait down to Cape Cod in the western North Atlantic There is also a record of white-sided dolphins near Virginia and in the Hudson River Canyon. In the eastern North Atlantic, they are found from Trondheim Fjord, Norway, southward to Ireland, the northern shores of England, and the Netherlands.

White-beaked Dolphin, *Lagenorhynchus albirostris.* This dolphin is always identified by a white or pale gray beak and two sweeping bands of pale gray on its dark side with one band in front of, and the other one below and behind, the prominent dorsal fin. It has a maximum length of 10 feet (3.1 meters); flippers and flukes are pointed, and the dorsal fin is high and falcate. There are 22 to 28 teeth in each side of the upper and lower jaws.

Confined to colder regions of the Atlantic, its range includes the North Sea, northern Norway, Greenland, the Davis Strait, and Cape Cod. In these swift currents, the dolphins gather in random groups, or larger herds that may number up to fifteen hundred, to follow migrating schools of cod, herring, and capelin. Close to the ocean floor, they hunt for snails, hermit crabs, whelks, or octopuses, and pursue the gossamer forms of squid through the dim light of deep waters. White-beaked dolphins are insulated from the frigid waters of the far North Atlantic by thick layers of blubber that underlie their thin skins. Young dolphins, 3.6 feet (1.1 meters) in length, are born during the summer in northern feeding grounds.

Species of *Lagenorhynchus:* from top, Pacific white-sided dolphin, *L. obliquidens;* Atlantic white-sided dolphin, *L. acutus;* white-beaked dolphin, *L. albirostris.*

SPECIES OF *LAGENORHYNCHUS*

Dusky Dolphin, *Lagenorhynchus obscurus.* The dusky dolphin is similar in form to the Pacific white-sided dolphin, but its beak is somewhat longer, the flippers are blue-gray, and the dorsal fin is less falcate, with a deep indigo leading edge shading to blue-gray. Its back is dark indigo-gray, and the belly is white with a faint blue-gray line stretching from the flipper to encircle the eye and end at the beak. On its side, the dolphin has two wide white stripes extending upward toward the moderately large dorsal fin. Overall length is approximately 4.5 to 7 feet (1.4 to 2 meters), and teeth number from 24 to 36 in each side of the upper and lower jaws. Large schools of dusky dolphins gather to pursue squid and fish in the waters near New Zealand and the Falkland Islands, but these groups apparently do not venture south of 58° south latitude. There are scattered populations distributed in more temperate waters flowing near South America, New Zealand, the ocean near southern Australia, South Africa, and around the Kerguelen Islands. *L. obscurus* is also called Fitzroy's dolphin and the southern striped dolphin.

Hourglass Dolphin, *Lagenorhynchus cruciger.* Color has transformed this dolphin into a splendid, conspicuous figure: from beak to tail flukes, the back is black and the belly white, with the dorsal fin, flippers, and flukes ranging from dark gray to black. On the sides, a black band leads from eye to flipper, then widens, hourglass fashion, below the large, falcate dorsal fin, narrowing again until it reaches the flukes. Racing through sunlit waters, *L. cruciger* resembles the Pacific white-sided dolphin but is smaller, measuring 5 to 6 feet (1.6 to 1.8 meters) in length. Its dorsal fin is falcate and its short beak has a count of 28 pairs of sharp, curved teeth lining the upper jaw and 24 pairs lining the lower jaw. Hourglass dolphins roam the sea lanes of the southern hemisphere in the cool waters and strong currents of the West Wind Drift. They are found above and below the rich feeding grounds of the Antarctic Convergence, a band of water 28 miles wide circling Antarctica between 50° and 60° latitude where the frigid water of Antarctica flowing north encounters warm water flowing south with subsequent upwelling of deep, mineral-rich currents. The dolphins also occur between 50° south and drifting floes from the pack ice of the Antarctic.

Peale's Dolphin, *Lagenorhynchus australis.* Inquisitive and playful, this dolphin reaches a length of 6.5 to 7 feet (2 to 2.1 meters). Its dorsal fin is moderately high and falcate, the flippers are small, and the flukes are thin with pointed tips. The upper part of its body, including the back, flippers, dorsal fin, flukes, and the head and eye area, is black, while the breast is gray and the belly white. A dark stripe runs from the base of the flippers to its mouth, and a broad white band stretches diagonally across the dark dorsal area from the caudal section up to and beyond the dorsal fin. Approximately 30 teeth line each side of the upper and lower jaws. Limited to South America, Peale's dolphin is found near the Strait of Magellan, Chile, Cape Horn, Argentina, and the Falkland Islands.

Species of *Lagenorhynchus:* from top, dusky dolphin, *L. obscurus;* hourglass dolphin, *L. cruciger;* Peale's dolphin, *L. australis.*

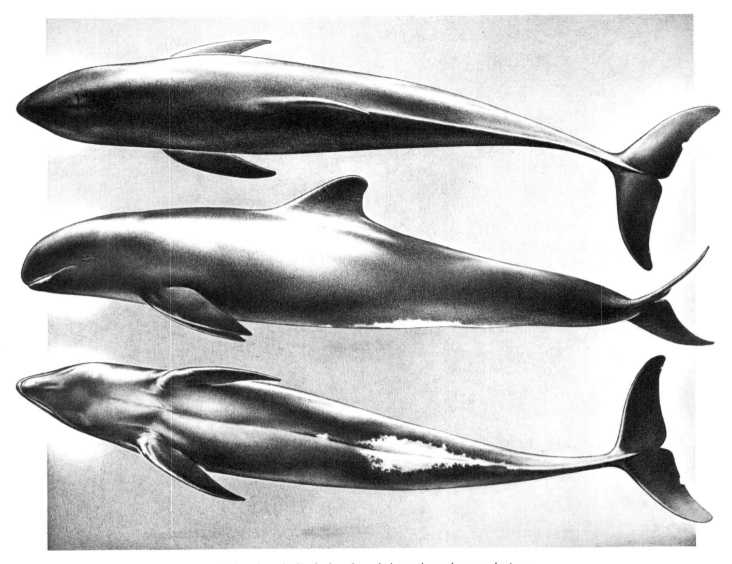

Melon-headed whale: dorsal, lateral, and ventral views.

Melon-headed Whale

Peponocephala electra

When a great storm moves over the ocean, gentle swells begin to deepen and the wind shifts erratically, then increases to gale force, racing low above foam capped water to be followed by lashing squalls of rain. Sometimes, in the trough of towering waves, a line of dark heads may appear, bobbing in the surge and pull of a heavy sea. Melon-headed whales, *Peponocephala electra,* often rest on the surface in a vertical position before they sink down into quiet depths, drifting lower until a soft green twilight surrounds them and all is still. Lulled by familiar sounds, the little whales sleep fitfully while the storm roars above and the ocean's surface heaves in the grip of violent winds.

Peponocephala has a blunt snout, narrow at the lip line, which curves upward and outward into a broad, rounded head. Its dorsal fin is moderately large and falcate, the flippers are long, and the flukes are wide. Males reach a length of approximately 9 feet (2.7 meters), while females are somewhat smaller. Color is muted: the body of a melon-headed whale is jet black, or a deep grayish black relieved by a thin band of white edging the upper and lower lip line, with other areas of white scattered over the ventral surface and a pale, anchor-shaped pattern appearing on its breast. While there is a confusing similarity to both the false killer whale (18 feet [5.5 meters]) and the long-finned pilot whale (22 feet [6.7 meters]), the melon-headed whale is obviously smaller (9 feet [2.7 meters]) and does not have a reversed curve on the leading edge of its flipper like the false killer whale, nor does it have a long, sickle-shaped flipper like the pilot whale.

In size, form, and color, however, the melon-headed whale bears an uncanny resemblance to the pygmy killer whale. The two can be separated by comparing flipper tips, semiround in pygmy killer whales and pointed in melon-headed whales, and also by a tooth count, with 10 to 13 pairs of teeth lining the upper and lower jaws of the pygmy killer whale, while the teeth of *Peponocephala* number 21 to 25 pairs in the upper jaw and 21 to 24 pairs in the lower jaw. This imposing array of teeth has caused the little whale to be called "many-toothed blackfish."

Although information is limited on *P. electra,* it is known to be gregarious, gathering in small, sociable groups numbering from three or four up to twenty, or collecting in a moderately large herd made up of one to five hundred members. In the Pacific, birth is thought to take place around early June, with very young whales observed in August. At this time, the melon-headed whale is found in the warm waters of temperate and tropical areas of the Indian, Pacific, and Atlantic oceans.

Range of melon-headed whales.

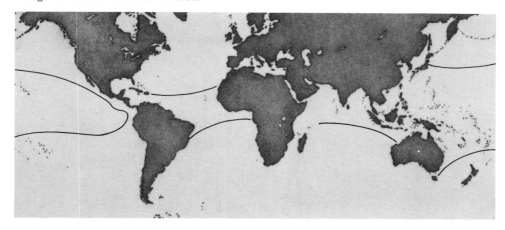

A solitary pygmy killer whale passing a group of manta rays.

Pygmy Killer Whale
Feresa attenuata

In 1963, a group of fourteen small, black whales was overtaken by fishermen from Izu Peninsula, Japan. The whales were slow-moving and appeared to be manageable, so the fishermen drove them approximately thirty miles to their village, where the docile creatures were placed in a holding pen. Examined by Masaharu Nishiwaki and found to be a new type of whale, the captives were purchased by the Ito Aquarium and transferred to the aquarium's pool.

Various foods, such as sauries, mackerel, sardines, and squid, were offered, but all the whales, with the exception of one, refused to eat and died. The single individual lingered for twenty-one days before dying of acute pneumonia. These were the first living specimens of the pygmy killer whale, *Feresa attenuata,* to be recorded.

The whales were described as relatively slender, with the maximum length of males listed at 8 feet (2.4 meters) and females at 7 feet (2.2 meters). Rounded and beakless, the shape of the head and body resembled that of a false killer whale. A tall dorsal fin, placed near the midpoint of the back, was triangular and slightly falcate, similar to the fin of a bottlenose dolphin, while flippers were longer, with a moderately rounded tip. There were approximately 10 to 13 teeth lining each side of the upper and lower jaws. A description of color indicated the small whale was dark gray or black above, blackish gray on the sides, and often displayed a white zone from navel to anus on its gray underside. A narrow band of white lined the lips, and on its breast a pale anchor-shaped pattern sometimes appeared between the flippers. According to Nishiwaki, there was an irregular, light striping on its sides that faded after the whale died and eventually disappeared completely when its skin dried.

Although they were small and seemingly harmless, aggressive behavior toward other captives was noted in the aquarium's whales. Indeed, when a pygmy killer whale approached a group of dolphins, there was a sudden silence and an abrupt cessation of play as the dolphins gathered into a tight cluster, obviously disturbed and eyeing the slim, black form with apprehension. Such a clear fright reaction when confronted by *Feresa attenuata* suggests that this small whale may attack and kill other dolphins.

While little information has been obtained on breeding or birth, there was one instance of a possible newborn pygmy killer whale, found near Costa Rica, which measured 32 inches (82.2 centimeters) in length. *Feresa,* also known as the slender blackfish and slender pilot whale, is seldom encountered and apparently is limited to tropical or temperate waters in widely separated areas of the world. It is found in the temperate and tropical waters of the Atlantic, Pacific, and Indian oceans.

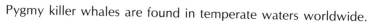

Pygmy killer whales are found in temperate waters worldwide.

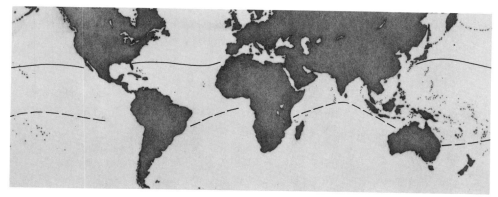

Commerson's dolphin, one of the most beautiful little cetaceans in the southern hemisphere.

Commerson's Dolphin
Cephalorhynchus commersonii

The Strait of Magellan divides the southern tip of South America, forming a sea corridor of considerable depth from the Atlantic to the Pacific oceans. Far down in the dark waters that move through this channel, a forest of kelp grows upward toward the surface light, lifting a wilderness of great, brown blades, or leaves, attached to slender stems that sway in rhythm to the ebb and flow of heavy tides. These strands of seaweed, sometimes 100 feet (30 meters) long, are anchored to massive boulders on the bottom by corded, holdfast roots. It is in this deep corridor and around the tip of South America that one of the most beautiful dolphins in the southern hemisphere makes its home.

Commerson's dolphin, *Cephalorhynchus commersonii,* is small and plump, with an overall length ranging up to 6 feet (1.8 meters). Its beak, indicated by a slight depression at the base of the forehead, has 29 to 30 sharp teeth lining each side of the upper and lower jaws. Its dorsal fin, distinctly rounded and rising midway along the back, is connected to a very low dorsal ridge that extends toward the flukes; the flippers are oval, and the flukes have a semicrescent shape with a small median notch. The forepart of its body, including head and flippers, is jet black with an oval white patch covering both chin and throat. The center section of the body is pure white, broken by an oval black spot on the underside, while the rear part of the body, from dorsal fin to flukes, is solid black. This handsome pattern of black, separated by a wide band of white, may act as a camouflage by dividing the dolphin's body into separate parts in order to deceive packs of killer whales and other enemies that wander near the tip of South America and the turbulent currents of the West Wind Drift. Such camouflage is thought to be most successful when the dolphins are feeding among broken slabs of ice that drift out from Antarctica.

Descending as deep as 600 feet (100 fathoms), they search the great forests of kelp in the strait and the waters of coastal areas, with some groups venturing out into the surge of the Cape Horn Current to follow and feed on squid and fish. Closer to the surface, they skim through thick concentrations of euphausiids that swarm in the upper levels of the Antarctic Ocean.

Sometimes called the piebald porpoise or *le jacobite,* Commerson's dolphin is abundant around the southern tip of South America from Peninsula Valdés (42° south latitude), on the coast of Argentina, south to the Cape Horn Current, and on the coast of Chile from 53° south latitude down to the center of the Drake Passage. Small groups are found near the Falkland Islands, South Georgia Islands and, according to one report, the Kerguelen Islands.

At the present time, three additional species are listed under the genus *Cephalorhynchus:* these include Heaviside's dolphin, *C. heavisidii;* the black dolphin, *C. eutropia;* and Hector's dolphin, *C. hectori.*

Limited range of Commerson's dolphin.

SPECIES OF *CEPHALORHYNCHUS*

Commerson's Dolphin, *Cephalorhynchus commersonii* (**A**). This handsome black-and-white dolphin varies from 4.5 to 6 feet (1.37 to 1.8 meters) in length. Thriving on fish, squid, and krill, it is found near the Strait of Magellan, the southern coastal areas of South America, and the remote Kerguelen Islands (one report).

Heaviside's Dolphin, *Cephalorhynchus heavisidii* (**B**). With a maximum length listed at 4 feet (1.3 meters), Heaviside's dolphin is one of the smallest species on record. A broadly triangular dorsal fin is situated near the midpoint of its back, the flippers are slender and rounded at the tip, and the tail flukes have a concave rear edge. Like other species of *Cephalorhynchus,* the dolphin has a pointed snout and a lower jaw that extends beyond the upper one. Lining each side of the upper and lower jaws, are 25 to 30 sharp little teeth that are used efficiently when pursuing squid and bottom fishes in the coastal waters of the Benguela Current flowing between Cape Cross, Namibia, and Cape Town, South Africa. The arrangement of color on Heaviside's dolphin is conspicuous, with black and white areas sharply divided. Its head and back are jet black, flippers and flukes are black above, and the underside of the body, from its throat to the base of its flukes, is marked with pure white in a lobed pattern similar to the killer whale: only a white eyespot is missing.

The name "Heaviside" is a mistake that may have occurred in 1827 when Captain Haviside placed a collection of cetacean anatomical specimens on sale in London, at the same time that a prominent surgeon, Captain Heaviside, was selling a collection of noncetacean anatomical specimens—and the original error in spelling Haviside's name may have been made.

Black Dolphin, *Cephalorhynchus eutropia.* Sometimes called the Chilean dolphin, *C. eutropia* is very small, reaching a length of around 4 feet (1.4 meters). Its flippers are short, the dorsal fin is rounded, and the flukes have a decided curve on the posterior edge. Approximately 28 to 31 pairs of teeth line the upper and lower jaws. Basic body color is dark gray with areas of white on the throat, behind the flippers, and on the belly. This rare and very shy dolphin is restricted to the coast of Chile, from the fjord region at Isla Navarino up to Concepción.

Hector's Dolphin, *Cephalorhynchus hectori* (**C**). *C. hectori* resembles Heaviside's dolphin, but the upper part of its body is pale to medium or dark gray, deepening to black at the border of the white ventral area. There is a white or gray forehead patch and a black genital spot. Adult length is 5 to 6 feet (1.5 to 1.8 meters). On this dolphin, the head is longer and the slightly defined beak contains 30 to 32 teeth in each side of the upper and lower jaws. Its low dorsal fin is rounded, the flukes are small, and the flippers have an odd shape, with both sides being almost parallel down to a rounded tip. Confined to the coastal waters of New Zealand, groups of these dolphins feed on anchovies or other small fish in areas close to shore.

Species of *Cephalorhynchus:* from top, Commerson's dolphin, *C. commersonii;* Heaviside's dolphin, *C. heavisidii;* Hector's dolphin, *C. hectori.*

Dolphins: from top, killer whale, false killer whale, and Irrawaddy dolphin.

Dolphins, Delphinidae (continued)

KILLER WHALE
OTHER COMMON NAME: orca
GENUS: *Orcinus*
SPECIES: killer whale, *Orcinus orca,* the single species

FALSE KILLER WHALE
OTHER COMMON NAMES: lesser killer whale, false killer
GENUS: *Pseudorca*
SPECIES: false killer whale, *Pseudorca crassidens,* the single species

IRRAWADDY DOLPHIN
OTHER COMMON NAME: Irrawaddy River dolphin
GENUS: *Orcaella*
SPECIES: Irrawaddy dolphin, *Orcaella brevirostris,* the single species

Killer whales spiraling down to surround a school of tuna.

Killer Whale
Orcinus orca

Bold, aggressive, and powerful, the killer whales, *Orcinus orca,* are the largest members of the dolphin family. They are the greatest carnivores on earth and the most highly organized predators in the ocean. Shrewd and dominant, they fear few living things. As hunters, these handsome whales are superb. The movements of a hunting pack appear to be so thoroughly coordinated that success is almost assured. In search of food, young bulls and juveniles forage through relatively shallow areas along the coast to hunt for schooling fish, while older and heavier bulls, seeking larger prey, range farther out, in deeper waters. Dolphins are sometimes trapped by the whales, but usually avoid an encounter because their sonar gives early warning of approaching danger. If a school of tuna is located, however, the killer whales quickly surround the area, spiraling down to close on their target in a narrowing circle that revolves around the milling fish until they can be seized one by one. Few escape this deadly encirclement, and any tuna that attempt to streak away near the surface must face yet another test. Pursuing these fast-moving fish on the surface, the whales are said to cover 40 to 43 feet (12 to 13 meters) in one great leap.

The most conspicuous feature of a killer whale is a prominent dorsal fin that rises midway on its back. Tall, slender, and triangular, this fin displays wide variation in shape: the leading edge may be perpendicular or curved, and the tip may be sharply pointed, slanted, or falcate. The whale's body is stout, showing maximum girth at the dorsal fin, with a more slender caudal section tapering gradually toward the flukes. The paddle-like flippers are

Varied forms of the dorsal fin.

large, oval, and rounded at the tip; while the flukes, measuring approximately one fifth of body length, are very strong. Male orcas display a remarkable increase in the size of all appendages as they become older; their flippers and flukes show enormous growth and the black dorsal fin often rears its tall pinnacle upward as far as 6.5 feet (2 meters). There is also a marked difference in overall measurement between male and female orcas. Males reach an average length of 27 feet (8.2 meters), while females are 23 feet (7 meters), with maximum lengths extending to 31 feet (9.4 meters) and 27 feet (8.2 meters), respectively. The orca's snout is blunt and its mouth is wide, structured with strong bone and lined on each side of the upper and lower jaws with 10 to 12 large teeth which interlock firmly when the mouth is closed.

Color is distinctive in the killer whale. A design of intense black and white in sharp contrast, divided by flowing curves, has produced an unusually beautiful effect. The back and sides are separated from immaculate white underparts by a demarcation line sweeping from snout to flukes in a wavelike pattern that skillfully disguises the body outline. Above the eye, there is a large, oval white spot, and immediately behind the dorsal fin an indistinct saddle of gray lies across the back. The upper and lower surfaces of the flippers are black, but the flukes usually show a white underside bordered with black.

Like other members of the dolphin family, orcas are seldom solitary, usually traveling in family groups or gathering in small bands of twenty-five to thirty, with reports from Iceland listing as many as fifteen hundred whales assembled to form a hunting pack. Although information is limited on the migration of killer whales, records have indicated they are frequently found in waters within 500 miles (800 kilometers) of land and appear to favor the colder regions of the northern and southern hemispheres.

A review of food items has suggested a preference, in some areas, for tuna, flatfish, skipjack, cod, and various types of schooling fishes. When searching for mullet or shad, the whales do not hesitate to enter coastal waters and may penetrate far inland on large rivers to invade interior lakes. One young whale, intent on chasing salmon, eventually ran aground in shallow water 30 miles (47 kilometers) upriver. Among larger fish, it is interesting to note that sharks of all types, prowling the coast or in the open sea, are pursued and captured by orcas; even a great white shark is not immune from attack. In the Antarctic, flocks of penguins and other sea birds are chased, and cephalopods, such as the swarms of squid that gather in the middle depths, are avidly followed; but octopuses are seldom eaten, perhaps because they are solitary and do not assemble in large numbers.

In spring, when groups of killer whales reach the drift ice of northern waters, they examine each large slab for harp seals or hooded seals, which like to loaf on the sun-warmed surface. Small ice cakes and pans are not safe, but young seals often attempt to bask on these little flat-topped blocks until the floating platforms are suddenly shattered by orcas and the wildly darting seals must swim for their lives. Older seals find shelter in the subterranean hollows and deep fractures of large icebergs; a wise precaution, because even

The food of killer whales includes fish, penguin, squid, sea otter, young walrus, seal, porpoise, dolphin, and whale.

A triumphant hunter.

heavy rafts of ice may offer little protection. Killer whales forcibly ram these brittle structures, battering them from below, using their broad backs to crack and splinter great blocks of ice 3.3 feet (1 meter) thick.

Throughout the Arctic, a pattern of caution appears to prevail when the rhythmic sounds of distant orcas are detected. Both white whales and narwhals leave open waters and vanish into shallow coastal areas or into the white obscurity of narrow leads, concealing themselves in these slush-filled openings that appear between splitting icebergs. Solitary seals also use this simple strategy, but large colonies must contend with more severe hazards. During the summer in the Bering Sea, roving bands of orcas gather near barren rock coasts where the breeding grounds of seals and sea lions have been established. They haunt the vicinity, alert for arriving or departing seals, patrolling the outer perimeter with such obvious intent that a bull Steller sea lion weighing 2,500 pounds (1,100 kilograms) is often hesitant about venturing far from the safety of the rocks. He has reason to pause and consider: in a sportive humor, killer whales have been known to dive close beneath seals swimming on the surface; then, striking upward with their powerful flukes, they send the hapless creature spinning high into the air; in a similar manner, giant tuna are tossed far above the surface by playful orcas.

The massive skull and formidable teeth of *Orcinus orca*.

Even the great whales are not spared. When one of these is located, a pack of orcas will surround their quarry, darting in to bite its lips or leaping on its back and blowhole. So great is the fear engendered by the hunters that, when confronted by advancing orcas, a gray whale may go into shock and roll belly up on the surface, insensible to pain. There are also displays of courage. Faced with imminent danger, a mother gray whale often saves herself and her calf by racing toward the shoreline, pressing through a jungle of kelp until her flukes touch bottom in very shallow water.

In killer whales, there is a mysterious reversal of aggressive behavior where humans are concerned; they appear to accept people as equal companions in their marine environment. Although there are no documented reports of deliberate injury or killing of humans, any person near these magnificent creatures should be aware of their tremendous power to inflict injury: everyone should treat killer whales with respect and refrain from provoking them in any way.

Reports from a large population of orcas in the Pacific Ocean off the coast of British Columbia and Washington State indicate most of the courtship

Two whales in spying position.

Adult whales supporting
a wounded little whale.

activity occurs in spring and summer, followed within thirteen to sixteen months by the birth of infants approximately 7 to 8 feet (2.1 to 2.4 meters) in length. A small killer whale is a miniature copy of its parents, with the rounded form and appealing charm of an infant. The single difference in color is a tan or yellow tint of the white areas. A life span ranging from twenty-five years up to a possible eighty-five years of age has been estimated for these whales.

Caregiving behavior has been observed, and there is evidence of a deep attachment between adults and young in a family group. One remarkable example of devotion *(National Geographic,* December 1976) took place near British Columbia when the captain of a ferryboat, intent on steering around a pair of killer whales, felt a bump near the propeller section. Looking back, he found a small killer whale had been injured by the propeller. As it rolled over in the water and sank, two adult whales dived to reach the infant and, side by side, lifted it to the surface and held it securely in the hollow of their two backs, although the large male appeared to have difficulty in maintaining his position. Fifteen days after this accident, a tourist passing through the same area reported seeing two large killer whales supporting a little whale in the hollow of their backs.

The population of orcas is widespread, but they are nowhere abundant. In recent years, five areas are known where these handsome whales gather in large numbers: the eastern and western coasts of the North Pacific, the North Atlantic, and the continent of Antarctica. No other whale is so widely dispersed or so well known throughout the world as the legendary killer whale.

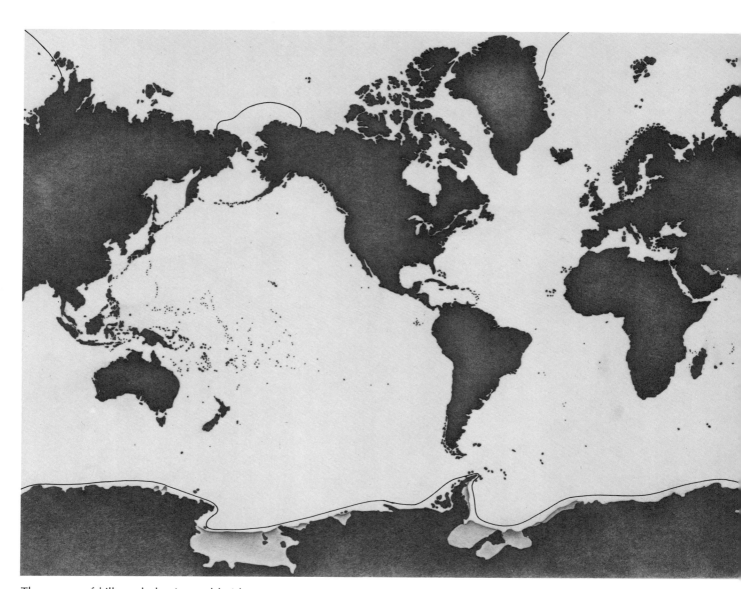

The range of killer whales is worldwide.

False killer whales entering the Bay of Kiel.

False Killer Whale
Pseudorca crassidens

The mist-shrouded fens of Lincolnshire lie on the eastern edge of England in an area where surging tides from the dark North Sea break over a rugged coastline. It was there, in 1843, that the subfossil skull of an unknown whale was discovered in a marsh area and sent to Sir Richard Owen. After extensive study, the specimen was pronounced to be extinct "until it shall be proved that it still exists in our seas." The required proof was provided sixteen years later when a school of approximately one hundred strange black whales beached themselves inside the Bay of Kiel, on the north coast of Germany. In this manner, the false killer whale, *Pseudorca crassidens,* was established in the list of living cetaceans.

Long-bodied and slenderly built, *Pseudorca* has a round head, a blunt snout, a falcate dorsal fin placed near the midpoint of the back, and slender, pointed flippers that have a definite reversed curve on the leading edge. Their caudal section is noticeably extended, and their flukes are moderately wide. The overall length of *Pseudorca* is approximately 18 to 20 feet (5.5 to 6 meters) for males and 16 feet (4.8 meters) for females.

The entire body is black, relieved by a faintly grayish chest area and a splendid set of teeth that gleam with intense whiteness against the whale's ebony skin. Large and sharply pointed, these teeth number from 8 to 12 pairs in the upper and lower jaws. Armed with such an impressive array, this big black whale is equipped to capture prey of very large size; in recent years, there have been reports of attacks by *Pseudorca* on small dolphins when they were released from the purse seines of tuna-fishing fleets.

In deep waters along the continental shelf, groups of false killer whales feed on schools of squid and migrating fish. Unfortunately, they have a taste for tuna, haddock, mackerel, cod, and other favorite food types collected by the fleets of commercial fisheries. Records from the East China Sea, the North Pacific Ocean, and the Atlantic Ocean report the stealing of fish from the hooks of longline fishing boats by wandering schools of false killer whales, which results in large herds of the whales being driven ashore in Japan and slaughtered by angry fishermen.

Once considered rare, members of *P. crassidens* are now known to gather in schools that number from two hundred up to several thousand individuals. These large assemblies are made up of males and females of all ages following the seasonal drift of squid as they roam the warm oceans in winter. Intent on pursuing fish or squid, they have been known to enter zones that are potentially dangerous.

In the past fifty years, false killer whales have appeared near shore in large numbers, often advancing into deceptively calm waters covering vast sand shelves or mud flats that extend down into the sea on such a gradual slope that, at high tide, there is enough deep water to float the largest whales. When the tidal flow reverses, however, and begins to withdraw from coastal regions, these flat slopes are drained of water so rapidly that large numbers of feeding whales may be trapped at low tide and become mired down in the wet sand or mud. Records covering the past century indicate these whales may beach themselves deliberately, coming ashore in small groups or assemblies numbering up to three hundred, all struggling onto a sandy beach moistened by receding waves, to lie in long, uneven rows of silent, black forms slowly dying of exposure and dehydration.

A problem in distinguishing between the melon-headed whale, the pygmy killer whale, and the false killer whale often occurs. All three are black, long-bodied, blunt-nosed whales of almost identical appearance, but each can be identified by size, shape, or color. Melon-headed whales have a maximum

P. crassidens following a school of squid.

Remarkable resemblance of the melon-headed whale, pygmy killer whale, and false killer whale. (Figures are not proportional.)

length of 9 feet (2.8 meters), a slate-gray belly, white lips, rounded dorsal fin, and pointed flippers. Pygmy killer whales have a maximum length of 8 feet (2.5 meters), white lips, a white belly patch, falcate dorsal fin, and flippers with a semiround tip. False killer whales have a maximum length of 20 feet (6 meters), a slender body form, rounded snout, falcate dorsal fin, and long recurved flippers.

Although little is known about the reproductive cycle of *Pseudorca,* there is some indication that breeding may extend over a considerable period of time, perhaps occurring throughout the year, with calves measuring approximately 5 to 7 feet (1.5 to 2.1 meters) long at birth. False killer whales are considered to be a pelagic, or deep-sea, species worldwide in distribution, roaming all the world's oceans with the exception of the frigid waters of the Arctic and Antarctic.

False killer whales roam temperate and tropical oceans worldwide.

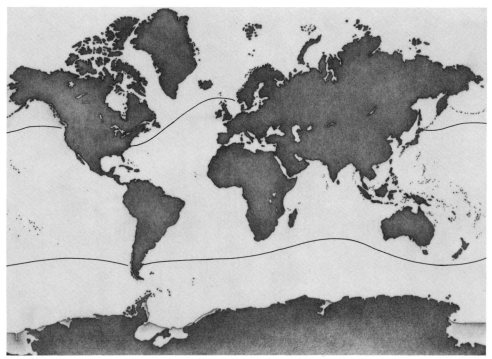

Irrawaddy dolphins searching among seaweed for crab and shrimp.

Irrawaddy Dolphin
Orcaella brevirostris

Placid in manner and gentle in disposition, the Irrawaddy dolphin, *Orcaella brevirostris,* is a sleepy-eyed little creature that wanders through the broad rivers and warm, gray-green seas of southern Asia. It is small, approximately 7 feet (2.1 meters) long. The head is round and beakless, with well-developed eyes, a crescent-shaped blowhole displaced slightly to the left, a flexible neck, and a mouth containing 12 to 19 tiny teeth lining each side of the upper and lower jaws. In young dolphins, these teeth are sharply pointed, but in older individuals, they may show considerable wear. The flippers are rather large and paddle-shaped, flukes are moderately broad, and the dorsal fin, small and falcate, is situated past the midline, with a low dorsal ridge extending back to the flukes. Instead of the fused vertebrae found in most dolphins, both the neck and tail vertebrae of *Orcaella* are remarkably flexible, allowing considerable freedom of movement. Color is limited to blue-gray or dark-gray on its back and sides, fading to a lighter shade below.

Rarely seen alone, Irrawaddy dolphins travel in groups of three to ten that journey by slow stages through the Ganges, Brahmaputra, Mekong, and other major rivers of southern Asia, with many venturing far inland on the Irrawaddy River to a point almost 900 miles (1,440 kilometers) from the sea. For dolphins that appear slow-moving, they pursue small fish with unexpected speed along the river bottom, or press through long-stemmed reeds and trailing water plants that border pebble beds and sandbars to search for crustaceans, capturing their quarry with limber skill.

Irrawaddy dolphins prefer fresh water or areas of low salinity. They are found in the warm, tropical regions of southern Asia from inshore or coastal waters in the Bay of Bengal, down through the Strait of Malacca, past Indonesia and Borneo up to the China Sea. In recent years, their range was found to be more extensive than previously known when they appeared far south of their recorded territory.

The great reefs around Australia conceal many deadly forms of life, from poisonous marine snakes to the diaphanous tentacles of small sea wasps and the barbs of motionless stonefish; but far more dangerous are the sharks that patrol the dark reefs and sunlit, sandy beaches. To control this menace, the beaches now are guarded by a series of gill nets which enmesh and kill any probing sharks. Unfortunately, dolphins sometimes fall prey to these nets. One report cites the capture of a female Irrawaddy dolphin in one of the shark nets placed near Townsville, Queensland, thus extending the range of *O. brevirostris* to Australia and the entire area of the northern end of the Great Barrier Reef.

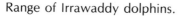
Range of Irrawaddy dolphins.

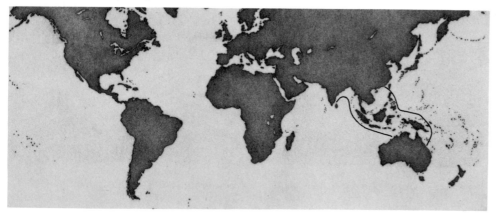

Dolphins: from top, long-finned pilot whale, northern right whale dolphin, and Fraser's dolphin.

Dolphins, Delphinidae (continued)

LONG-FINNED PILOT WHALE
OTHER COMMON NAMES: blackfish, pothead whale
GENUS: *Globicephala*
SPECIES: The genus *Globicephala* contains two species:
Long-finned pilot whale, *Globicephala melaena*
Short-finned pilot whale, *Globicephala macrorhynchus*

NORTHERN RIGHT WHALE DOLPHIN
OTHER COMMON NAME: none
GENUS: *Lissodelphis*
SPECIES: The genus *Lissodelphis* contains two species:
Northern right whale dolphin, *Lissodelphis borealis*
Southern right whale dolphin, *Lissodelphis peronii*

FRASER'S DOLPHIN
OTHER COMMON NAME: Bornean dolphin (old name)
GENUS: *Lagenodelphis*
SPECIES: Fraser's dolphin, *Lagenodelphis hosei,* the single species

A ghostly procession of little squid glides through blue-green depths, menaced by shadowy pilot whales.

Female squid
attaching egg cases.

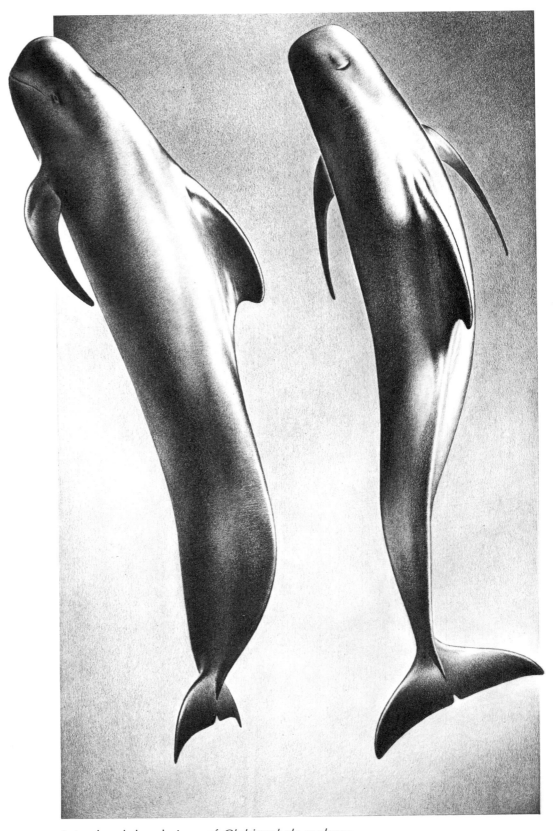

Lateral and dorsal views of *Globicephala melaena.*

Long-finned Pilot Whale
Globicephala melaena

In spring, great numbers of delicate little squid leave the deeper and darker regions of the ocean to ascend the long slopes of offshore banks. Pale ivory, pink, or gray, they stream in ghostly procession through the blue-green depths in search of spawning grounds where they deposit clusters of frail, oval eggs. Moving close behind the darting rivers of squid and feeding on them as they flow across the continental shelf are the dark, graceful forms of long-finned pilot whales, *Globicephala melaena.*

The head of a pilot whale is round, with the melon, or forehead, curving up and out in a bulbous development that is remarkable. Females and immature males have a moderate rounding of the forehead, and young adult males show a more definite enlargement, but the melon of a large and very old male pilot whale will bulge out from the lip line in a massive enlargement that is characteristic of this genus.

Comparison of long-finned and short-finned pilot whales.

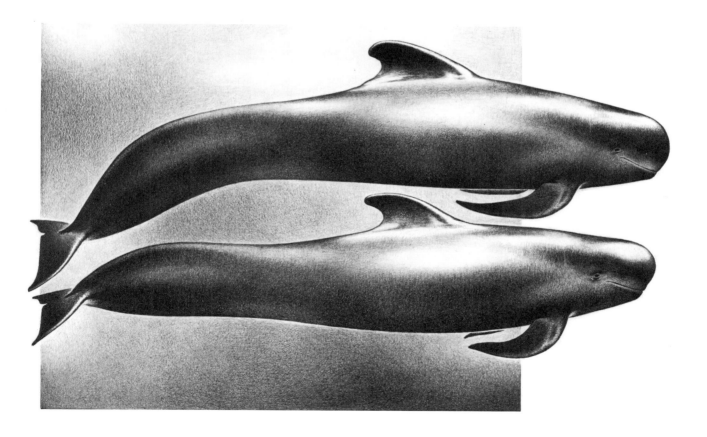

The body is robust and laterally compressed, with length ranging from 18 feet (5.5 meters) for females, up to a maximum of 20 feet (6.2 meters) for males. The dorsal fin is low, bluntly rounded, and falcate, rising from an extremely broad base placed far forward on the back. Flippers are extended into narrow, sickle-shaped fins equal to approximately one-fifth of body length, and the tail stock, which is very long, is laterally compressed and surmounted by a well-defined dorsal ridge ending at the flukes. Often called "blackfish," a pilot whale is jet black in color, with the exception of a light gray, anchor-shaped stripe extending from throat to abdomen and a reddish gray saddle which sometimes appears behind the dorsal fin. Calves are usually a lighter gray.

The migrations of pilot whales are governed by their food supply. In search of wandering squid, they form groups of four to fifty whales, sometimes assembling in hundreds or thousands of individuals that may remain in deep ocean areas through the winter, descending as far as 2,000 feet (600 meters) to feed on nocturnal cephalopods from the middle depths. Feeding usually takes place in the dark hours of night and early morning, when the whales gather over broad flats which serve as spawning grounds for shoals of small squid. Each whale dives down to pursue the flash of pale, darting forms, always positioned above and behind its quarry during the chase; when squid are no longer available, the whales hunt for flatfish, or follow Atlantic cod and mackerel. They have 8 to 11 pairs of strong teeth lining each jaw, and they seldom go hungry. Those remaining in the far North Atlantic during winter often feed on Greenland turbot.

It is thought that large herds are composed of many separate groups, each group made up of either juveniles or adult whales, with all very young whales swimming close to their mothers. Patrolling the perimeter, well out from the combined groups, are the old males. Beyond this widespread formation are schools of bottlenose, white-sided, and right whale dolphins, which accompany the pilot whales on their feeding forays and appear to profit from the whales' powerful sonar scanning, which sweeps a very broad area of ocean with penetrating sound waves. When a mass of squid is located, the whales dive and the smaller dolphins follow to capture a share of the feast.

The lives of these gentle whales are not without danger. The approach of killer whales will send them racing toward the nearest shore where some may be trapped by a receding tide and left to die of heat and dehydration. There is also the mysterious and unexplained phenomenon of deliberate stranding which occurs when a leader goes aground on a sloping beach, followed by other whales trying to aid him. Concern has been expressed over the fact that no proven cause for these mass strandings, or "suicides," has been found. In search of an answer, cetologists of the Smithsonian Institution have tested many beached whales for disease, but most of those examined appeared to be normal.

Mortality among males is reported to be much higher than among females. For this reason, males are in short supply and harems are maintained as a necessity. Courtship takes place in the warm waters of lower latitudes, and there is some indication that births may occur at any time of the year. The length of a newborn pilot whale is approximately 5 to 6 feet (1.6 to 1.8 meters).

The short-finned pilot whale, *Globicephala macrorhynchus,* a second species, was established in 1971 when an osteological examination by P. J. H. van Bree proved the genus *Globicephala* contained two clearly defined species, *G. melaena* and *G. macrorhynchus.* This whale attains a length of 15 feet (4.7 meters) for females and 19 feet (5.9 meters) for males. It is very similar to the long-finned pilot whale in form but has shorter flippers, limited to one-sixth of body length, and a count of 7 to 9 teeth in each side of the upper and lower jaws. With the exception of polar seas, pilot whales are found in oceans throughout the world.

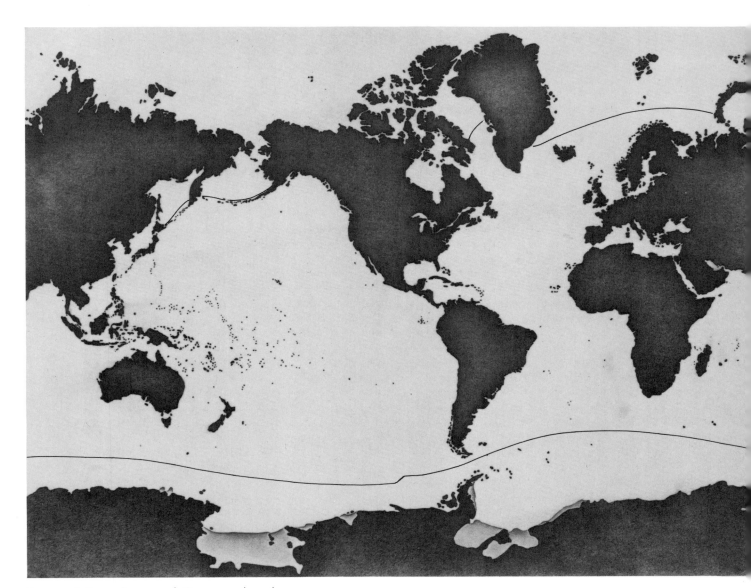

Range of *G. melaena* and *G. macrorhynchus.*

Northern right whale dolphins in pursuit of flying squid.

Northern Right Whale Dolphin
Lissodelphis borealis

In areas of the ocean where current rips occur, when two separate masses of oceanic waters flow parallel or in opposite directions, one fast and the other slow or one warm and the other cold, they roll up against each other and the surface is divided by a broad band of foam extending from one horizon to the other, with whitecaps marking the great shearing edges of the rip. In this boiling convergence, the water is often thick with plankton, squid, diving birds, sea turtles, and shoals of feeding fish, large and small. Scalloping through the whitecaps above this teeming abundance are black and white dolphins that have the shape of long, lean missiles. Northern right whale dolphins, *Lissodelphis borealis,* are very swift. In pursuit of little flying squid, such as the translucent and delicately colored cephalopods called "sea arrows," which rise to the surface at dusk, feeding dolphins will erupt into a series of rolling turns or high, spirited leaps, with jets of bright spray soaring upward and dark figures streaking away in all directions after the elusive, airborne quarry.

Extremely slender, sleek, and handsome, *Lissodelphis* reaches a maximum length of 10 feet (3 meters). Its short beak contains 37 to 46 pairs of sharply pointed teeth in the upper and lower jaws; the flippers are very narrow, tapering to a point; and the flukes are relatively small, with a deep notch in the posterior margin. There is no dorsal fin. In this dolphin, the back is a long, smooth, unbroken curve flowing from the base of its short beak to its flukes. The name "right whale dolphin" derives from the fact that both *Lissodelphis* and the great right whale, *Eubalaena,* have no dorsal fins rising above their flat backs. The upper part of the dolphin's body, including flippers and flukes, is an intensely deep black, which contrasts sharply with the brilliant white area appearing on the lower jaw and abdomen, widening between the flippers, then narrowing in hourglass fashion to a tenuous strip of white continuing down the lower caudal area to cover the outer edges of the flukes.

These are deepwater dolphins that usually spend their entire lives wandering across the limitless expanse of the oceans, far from any shores. They

Lateral, dorsal, and ventral views of the northern right whale dolphin.

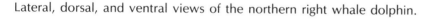

Lateral, dorsal, and ventral views of the southern right whale dolphin.

gather in groups of up to two hundred individuals, or assemble in vast herds of over two thousand dolphins to probe the dark green depths, sometimes schooling with mackerel or plunging down to pursue luminous blue lantern fish and the smaller species of squid and pelagic fish.

Enemies in the form of killer whales, sharks, and other predators sometimes follow the dolphins but are not always successful, because *Lissodelphis* reacts with great speed. When frightened, a group will take flight across the top of the water, slicing over the surface with low, arching leaps, each group separating to race away in different directions until a safe distance has been achieved, then regrouping. Right whale dolphins are reported to be extremely sensitive: When captured or held by a net, they become immobile, floating without movement as though in shock. Within days after their capture, many dolphins die, showing the classic symptoms of stress.

Although the habits of these dolphins are not well known, they apparently prefer relatively warm areas and do not wander into the extremely cold regions of the Arctic. In the eastern Pacific, *Lissodelphis borealis,* the northern right whale dolphin, ventures as far north as British Columbia or northern California and is commonly found in offshore waters from 50° north latitude down to San Clemente Island, with the largest numbers of dolphins reported from Point Sur down to the southern California Channel Islands. In the western Pacific, right whale dolphins are reported as far north as northern Honshu Island, Japan (41° north latitude).

The southern right whale dolphin, *Lissodelphis peronii,* takes the place of *L. borealis* south of the Tropic of Capricorn. These southern dolphins have a head and body length of around 6 to 8 feet (1.8 to 2.4 meters) and a pattern of black and white color that is distinctive and extremely beautiful. The back, flukes, and top of the head are jet black or bluish black, the flippers are oyster white, showing a definite gray pigmentation, while the beak, sides, and abdomen are pure white. Although little information is available on *L. peronii,* they are known to be abundant around Concepción, where they gather off the coast of Chile in companies that may number more than five hundred to six hundred individuals.

Limited to the South Pacific in distribution, southern right whale dolphins apparently prefer the waters of the West Wind Drift, a great ocean current (45° to 65° south latitude) that flows eastward around the continent of Antarctica. Moving at moderate speed, it passes through the Cape Horn Current, across the Atlantic, past the tip of Africa and the southern coast of Australia to the Cape Horn Current once more. These beautiful dolphins are commonly found from Australia, New Zealand, and Tasmania to Chile and are frequently sighted in the Humboldt and Falkland currents.

Ranges of northern and southern right whale dolphins.

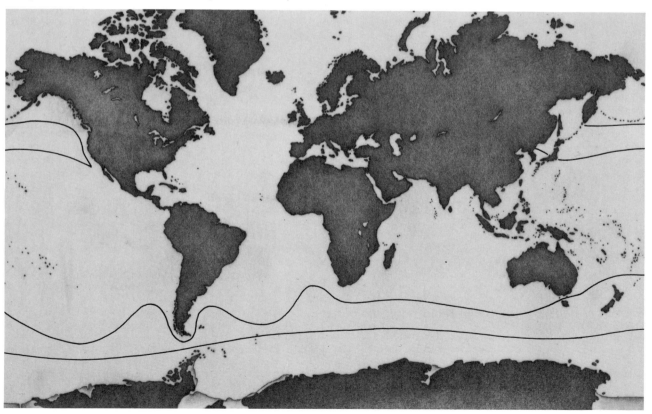

Dorsal, lateral, and ventral views of Fraser's dolphin, long considered extinct.

Fraser's Dolphin

Lagenodelphis hosei

For decades, mystery has surrounded the small cetacean that once was called the "Bornean dolphin." The first recorded evidence of its existence came from Baram Point, Sarawak Province, Borneo, before 1895, when the body of a strange dolphin was discovered on the bank of a river by Dr. Charles Hose. Measurements of this single specimen indicated a length of approximately 8 feet (2.4 meters). Named *Lagenodelphis hosei* by F. C. Fraser, its story might have ended with a labeled skull and assorted bones gathering dust in a drawer—but the unexpected happened and a new, far brighter chapter of study opened for *Lagenodelphis.*

In 1971, this dolphin, long considered extinct, suddenly appeared alive and thriving in the waters of the Pacific Ocean. According to records, it resembled the striped dolphin in form and, superficially, in color, but had a stout body, an extremely short beak, very small flippers, and a slender, falcate dorsal fin with a pointed tip. Examination of the newly discovered dolphin revealed a count of 40 to 44 teeth in each side of the upper jaw and 39 to 44 teeth lining each side of the lower jaw. The body was described as gray above and white below with a dominant pattern of three stripes—cream white, black, and cream white—running diagonally across the side from the juncture of the forehead and rostrum down to the ventral surface. Both the upper and lower surfaces of the flippers were listed as dark.

Given the common name of Fraser's dolphin, it was found to be extremely shy and difficult to approach. Reports have indicated that the dolphins assemble in groups ranging from a few individuals up to companies of around five hundred to hunt for food in waters distant from land. They dive down into a twilight zone and probably beyond into the darkness of lower depths to pursue the ghostly forms of agile little squid and various types of deep-sea fishes through the cold, echoing gloom. Their chase is swift, aggressive, and usually successful, with the dolphins streaking upward to surface in a whirl of white spray.

Recent observations have extended the range of Fraser's dolphin to the Phoenix Islands, Taiwan, South Africa (Indian Ocean), the waters between the Galápagos Islands and Central America, the central Pacific, and the eastern tropical Pacific. Records of stranded individuals have come from such distant lands as Japan, South Africa, and Australia, with a few dolphins captured alive in Philippine waters and displayed in oceanaria.

Probable range of Fraser's dolphin.

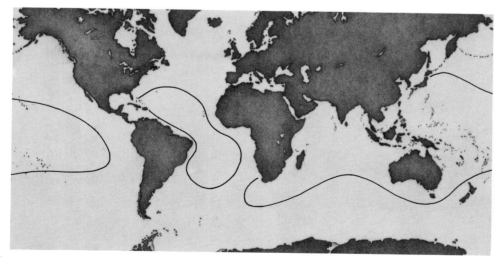

Porpoises: from top, harbor porpoise, Dall's porpoise, and the finless porpoise.

Porpoises, Phocoenidae

The porpoises are limited to three cetaceans called the harbor porpoise, Dall's porpoise, and the finless porpoise. All three are very small, ranging from 4.5 to 7 feet (1.5 to 2.1 meters) in length, with a stout body form, a round beakless head, a varied number of fused cervical vertebrae, and peculiar teeth which have placed them in a separate family called the Phocoenidae.

The most distinctive feature that divides porpoises from dolphins is the structure of their teeth. All other toothed whales and dolphins are equipped with cone-shaped teeth that have sharp points. The teeth of a porpoise are small and spade-shaped with flat or compressed crowns and are usually embedded in the gums, exposing only their blunt tops.

Harbor and finless porpoises are inshore and riverine species, wandering through harbors or sunny coastal waters and often ascending large inland rivers. Dall's porpoises, however, prefer offshore depths, roaming along the continental shelf and venturing over very deep areas in the North Pacific in a restless search for small fish and squid.

Listed below are the porpoises, their common names, classifications, and numbers of species.

HARBOR PORPOISE
    OTHER COMMON NAME: common porpoise
    GENUS: *Phocoena*
    SPECIES: The genus *Phocoena* contains four species:
        Harbor porpoise, *Phocoena phocoena*
        Cochito, *Phocoena sinus*
        Burmeister's porpoise, *Phocoena spinipinnis*
        Spectacled porpoise, *Phocoena dioptrica*

DALL'S PORPOISE
    OTHER COMMON NAME: Pacific porpoise
    GENUS: *Phocoenoides*
    SPECIES: Dall's porpoise, *Phocoenoides dalli,* the single species

FINLESS PORPOISE
    OTHER COMMON NAMES: black finless porpoise, Indian porpoise, Southeast Asia porpoise
    GENUS: *Neophocaena*
    SPECIES: finless porpoise, *Neophocaena phocaenoides,* the single species

Harbor porpoises search for schools of small fish in the green depths.

Harbor Porpoise
Phocoena phocoena

Drifting down through twilight depths toward a scalloped sand floor, two shadowy forms search for young herring and cod. They descend with the quick, graceful movements of dolphins; but these shy cetaceans are harbor porpoises, *Phocoena phocoena,* belonging to the family Phocoenidae, or porpoises, because they are structurally different from dolphins in several important features.

Instead of the conical, sharply pointed teeth of dolphins and toothed whales, the teeth of a harbor porpoise are spatulate, or spade-shaped, and are considered to be more complex. All porpoise teeth are described as short and peglike, topped by bluntly pointed crowns that scarcely penetrate the gums. As a porpoise ages, these crowns gradually wear down to the gum line, leaving a series of small dark stumps. Another point of difference is the fact that the backs of dolphins are smooth around the dorsal fin; in contrast, the backs of immature porpoises may display small horny denticles embedded on the anterior edge of the dorsal fin, at times continuing for a short distance along the back, particularly in Burmeister's porpoise. These denticles, resembling a line of indented beading; sometimes disappear with maturity.

Of the four species of *Phocoena*, the most familiar is the little harbor porpoise, short and plump, reaching a maximum adult length of approximately 6 feet (1.8 meters) and a weight of around 150 to 200 pounds (68 to 90 kilograms), with females slightly larger than males. *P. phocoena* has the round, beakless head of a true porpoise, a low, triangular dorsal fin, semioval flippers with blunt tips, and rather small flukes. The dorsal axillary girth is considered to be unusually wide, and the neck is reported to have up to six cervical vertebrae so firmly compressed that each vertebra appears to be mashed to a leaflike thinness. Its teeth, which resemble small, bulbous pegs, number approximately 23 to 28 in each side of the upper jaw, with 22 to 26 lining each side of the lower jaw.

The porpoise's head is very dark on top, changing abruptly to white below its eyeline, except for a dark tip on the lower lip. Its back is dark brown or a deep blue-gray, fading on the sides to a lighter grayish brown enhanced by a random pattern of tiny dark spots. On the underside, the gray-brown changes to a pale gray or pure white that extends up the sides in a wide band

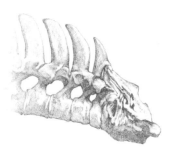

Compressed cervical vertebrae.

Indented tubercles on the dorsal fin.

The teeth of a porpoise have blunt crowns, while those of a dolphin are sharply pointed.

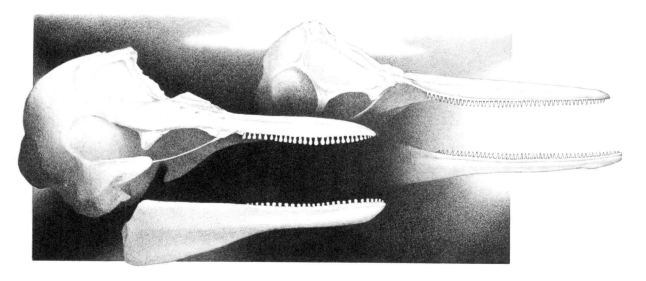

Pregnant porpoise and the folded position of an infant before birth.

immediately behind the flippers. The dorsal fin, flippers, and flukes are very dark, and a narrow black line leads from the base of each flipper to the angle of the mouth.

Traveling in pairs or in groups of five to ten, at times gathering in herds of more than one hundred porpoises, they descend as deep as 250 feet (75 meters) to follow the luminous flight of squid in the gloom of deeper gullies. When squid are scarce, they search for schools of young fish in the green depths, or hunt for small flatfish hiding in the sandy floor of a shelving coastline. Harbor porpoises show a preference for pollock, whiting, herring, sardines, and cod, but size is important, and they will chase and swallow only fish measuring less than 12 inches (30 centimeters) in length, because the small mouths of the porpoises always limit the size of their food. In spring and again in autumn, a new dimension is added to their nourishment when spawning fish enter shallow water to deposit roe. At this time, the porpoises gather around any large beds of seaweed they find and examine the stems carefully. Like the finless porpoise, *Neophocaena,* they are eager to feed on delicacies such as herring eggs attached to strands of seaweed, and they quickly strip any deposits of eggs from the plants.

Throughout the winter, these appealing little mammals thrive in temperate coastal waters, but in spring and summer, sometime between March and July, wandering groups assemble in favorite northern bays and broad estuaries to mate and bear their young. Courting pairs swim side by side, frequently stroking each other to the accompaniment of special sounds expressed during this ritual. In other areas, some of the females seek a quiet place to give birth to infant porpoises weighing approximately 14 to 22 pounds (6.4 to 10 kilograms) and measuring around 30 inches (75 centimeters) in length, almost half as long as their mothers. All unborn cetaceans, including porpoises, pass through eight to sixteen months of intensive development before birth in order to be prepared to exist in a rather hostile environment the minute they are born. To accommodate the increasing size of the unborn, nature has provided an adaptive procedure. As the months pass after conception, the developing fetus increases in length until a straight position can no longer be maintained within the abdominal capacity of the mother porpoise, forcing the fetus to curve into a folded shape and remain in this oval position until the time of birth is near, when it once more assumes a straight position and is born tail first, a process that protects the infant's head and blowhole until it is free of the mother's body and can surface to breathe.

Harbor porpoises, often called common porpoises, are found along the coastline of the North Atlantic Ocean from Iceland, Baffin Island, the White Sea, and the western coast of Greenland north of the Davis Strait, down to Cape Hatteras, North Carolina, in the west, and Senegal, Africa, in the east. Porpoises in the North Pacific Ocean area are recorded from the shores of Honshu and Hokkaido in the Sea of Japan up to the Bering Sea in the western section. In the eastern Pacific they are found from Santa Catalina, California, northward to the cold waters of Point Barrow, Alaska. Evidence of an isolated population has been discovered in the Black Sea, but the porpoises that once were numerous in the Baltic Sea are now decreasing as the parent stock is depleted by commercial fishing.

Apart from the harbor porpoise, there are three additional species of *Phocoena:* the cochito, *Phocoena sinus;* Burmeister's porpoise, *Phocoena spinipinnis;* and the spectacled porpoise, *Phocoena dioptrica.*

The range of harbor porpoises is worldwide in northern coastal waters.

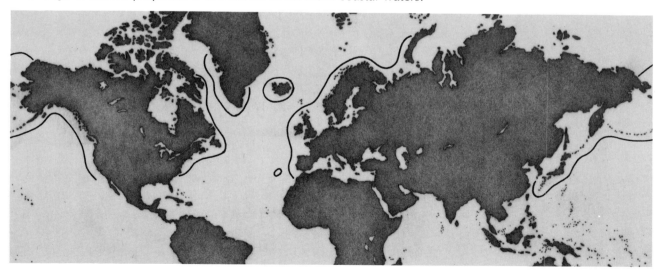

Harbor Porpoise, *Phocoena phocoena* (A). This porpoise ranges from 4.5 feet (1.3 meters) up to a maximum of 6 feet (1.8 meters) in length. Its body is plump, and its round, beakless head features a small mouth lined with blunt, spade-shaped teeth. Color is dark gray or brownish on top, shading to gray or white below. *P. phocoena* is widely distributed in the North Atlantic, the North Pacific, and the Mediterranean and Black seas.

Cochito, *Phocoena sinus*. The cochito, a relatively new species, was first described by Norris and McFarland in 1958. A single skull, discovered inside the Gulf of California on the Mexican coast, was found to be that of a very small adult porpoise with 18 to 21 pairs of teeth in each jaw. Two additional skulls recovered from the same area at a later date and the description of two female porpoises 4.5 feet (1.3 meters) and 5 feet (1.6 meters) in length appear to support the claim of a new species. Native fishermen report cochitos to be abundant in the upper region of the Gulf of California, where fish such as grunts and gulf croakers provide food.

Burmeister's Porpoise, *Phocoena spinipinnis* (B). Except for a narrow, white mid-ventral line and a pale area from chin to flipper insertion, Burmeister's porpoise is polished jet black in color, reaching a length of around 6 feet (1.9 meters) and a weight of 140 to 160 pounds (64 to 73 kilograms). The head is small, with 14 to 16 teeth on each side of the upper jaw and 17 to 19 teeth on each side of the lower jaw (Burmeister; see Allen, 1925). Its flippers are paddle-like, with a semioval tip; the flukes are narrow; and the dorsal fin is unique in structure, being low and reclining on the anterior edge and convex on the posterior edge, with a series of horny denticles appearing on the anterior edge. Often called the black porpoise, it is found along the Pacific coast of South America from Bahía de Paita, Peru, down to Valdivia, Chile, around the tip of Cape Horn and up the Atlantic coast to the province of Rocha, Uruguay.

Spectacled Porpoise, *Phocoena dioptrica* (C). The rare spectacled porpoise is a beautiful creature, clad in a combination of pure jet black on the upper body and brilliant white on the lower surface. There is a sharp demarcation line along the side, with white extending upward near the tail. Gray edges the white flippers and runs in a faint stripe from flipper to mouth, while black outlines the lips and encircles both eyes with black rims.

The average length of a male spectacled porpoise is around 6.6 feet (2 meters). The body is slender, with a blunt head, rounded dorsal fin, curved flippers, small flukes, and little spade-shaped teeth numbering 21 in each side of the upper jaw and 17 in each side of the lower jaw. It is found in the South Atlantic from Lagomar, Uruguay, down to Tierra del Fuego, at the tip of South America; the South Georgia Islands; the Falkland Islands; and, in the South Pacific, the Auckland Islands, near New Zealand.

Species of *Phocoena:* harbor porpoise, *P. phocoena;* Burmeister's porpoise, *P. spinipinnis;* spectacled porpoise, *P. dioptrica.*

Sober and restless, Dall's porpoises roam the North Pacific.

Dall's Porpoise
Phocoenoides dalli

They pass in single file, moving like shadows through the sunlit waters of northern seas, streaking swiftly up to the surface to breathe, then slicing back down beneath the waves. With each ascent, Dall's porpoises, *Phocoenoides dalli,* envelop themselves in great swirling fans of crystal spray. They are highly visible in a bold color pattern of brilliant black and white. The upper part of the body, including head, flippers, and flukes, is deep black. On the undersurface and sides, an area of pure white extends from behind the flippers to the caudal section, with a band of white edging the dorsal fin and outer margins of the flippers and flukes. Variations of this bicolor pattern include all-white and all-black porpoises in the Pacific Ocean.

Compact and powerful, Dall's porpoise reaches a maximum length of 6.75 feet (2.1 meters) and a weight of around 320 pounds (145 kilograms), with males slightly larger than females. It has a moderately small head, a dorsal fin that is high, triangular and broad-based, rather short flippers and powerful flukes. On the caudal section, remarkable keels form distinctive humps on both the dorsal and ventral surfaces.

The mouth is short with a slightly protruding lower jaw, and the teeth are spade-shaped and extremely small, numbering approximately 19 to 23 on each side of the upper jaw and 20 to 27 on each side of the lower jaw. Spaced between these tiny teeth, young porpoises have a series of peculiar bumps or horny plates that function as "gum teeth" in gripping squid and fish. As the porpoise matures, these plates usually wear away, leaving the small teeth unobstructed and useful.

Sober and restless, Dall's porpoises seem to lack the playfulness of most dolphins. They incessantly roam the sea-lanes, following large schools of

Diving down in a great, swirling plume of spray.

The color patterns of True's porpoise (upper) and Dall's porpoise (lower).

squid or fish, traveling at an aggressive, purposeful speed in small groups of two to twenty or assemblies of thousands. There has been some speculation that constant strenuous action may cause their hearts to enlarge. It is in the cold currents flowing through the southern Okhotsk and Bering seas, down to California that the young, measuring around 40 inches (90 centimeters) in length, are born sometime between July and August. Dall's porpoises are a northern species, limited to the cool waters of the North Pacific from the Bering Sea down to Baja California in the east and Choshi, Japan, in the west.

A subspecies, True's porpoise, *Phocoenoides truii,* differs slightly from Dall's porpoise in size, 6.8 feet (2.1 meters), and also in the distribution of black and white color, with the white area extending far forward on its sides beyond the flippers. These porpoises often travel with *P. dalli* in the temperate waters of the northwestern Pacific, where they follow shoals of migrating squid, and hunt for small, iridescent lantern fish which rise to the surface during the night. True's porpoise, now considered to be a form of *P. dalli,* will require extensive research and study to determine its status.

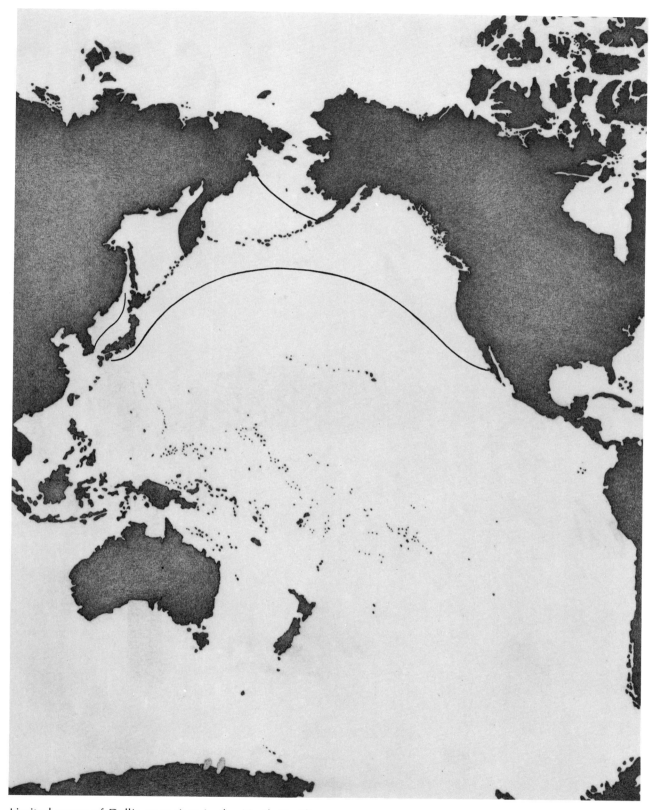

Limited range of Dall's porpoises in the North Pacific.

Finless porpoise carrying an infant on her back.

Finless Porpoise
Neophocaena phocaenoides

The back of the small finless porpoise, *Neophocaena phocaenoides,* curves in a smooth, unbroken line from the top of its round head to its flukes. In place of a dorsal fin, there is a long, narrow ridge extending down the back from the flipper line to near the flukes. This spinal ridge is bordered by rows of tiny denticles composed of hard, scale-like tissue that resemble the tubercles on the back of Burmeister's porpoise. A single row of these denticles is embedded in the back of the finless porpoise found in the Changjiang (Yangtze River), of China, and forms a resting place for infant porpoises clinging to their mothers. Cetologists who have witnessed this behavior report that the denticles surrounding the spinal ridge may help to hold the infant securely in place.

These curious scales also resemble those found on the dorsal fin of an immature harbor porpoise. Indeed, *Neophocaena* is thought to be the counterpart in Asia of the harbor porpoise, *Phocoena phocoena,* and has comparable measurements, reaching a length of 4.5 to 6 feet (1.4 to 1.8 meters). Its flippers are broad with a semipointed tip, and the flukes are rather wide, being equal to one fourth of total body length. Within its small mouth, there are 15 to 19 pairs of small spade-shaped teeth that line each jaw. Color ranges from pale bluish gray to light gray above, fading to a shadowy white on the underside, with a spotting of grayish white sometimes appearing on the throat and lips. Finless porpoises from India and Indonesia are described as very pale gray in color, while those found in the rivers of China and Japan are dark gray and often have no trace of spotting on throat or lips.

Skull of *N. phocaenoides.*

In Japanese waters, they travel in large companies of up to fifty porpoises that separate into groups of five to ten individuals. Moving at an easy pace, they search the river current or shallow zones near the coast for squid, shrimp and fish. Small cuttlefish, resting among strands of seaweed that grow in deeper areas, are choice fare for the porpoises. When clusters of fish eggs are found clinging to water plants, they move from one plant to another, stripping the eggs from their moorings, along with a few leaves. Among the types of fish consumed, sand lance is a favorite, and when a school is discovered, the porpoises completely surround the milling mass of fish and proceed to catch them one by one, feeding in a leisurely manner until all the fish are either consumed or have escaped to safety.

They journey by slow stages through many of the inland waterways of Asia and are reported to ascend the great Changjiang, penetrating far inland on its winding channel, passing beyond Poyang Lake, home of the baiji *(Lipotes vexillifer),* to reach Ichang Gorge, in far distant Hubei Province, a point approximately 1,000 miles (1,600 kilometers) from the mouth of the Changjiang.

The finless porpoise is a coastal and riverine species. Abundant in warmer inshore waters and widely distributed, its range extends from Pakistan and India down to Indonesia, Borneo, China and up to northern Japan.

Range of the finless porpoise.

The single species of Eschrichtidae is the gray whale.

Gray Whale, Eschrichtidae

The gray whale belongs to the Mysticeti, or great baleen whales, limited to those whales that have long plates of baleen, or whalebone, lining the upper jaw instead of teeth. The three families included in this category are represented by the gray whale, the balaenopterids, and the right whales.

In baleen whales, rudimentary tooth buds in the upper jaw of a fetus are absorbed before birth and replaced functionally by a permanent ridge of baleen. This modified tissue, which resembles thin blades of horn, lines the rim of the upper jaw in an orderly row of tough, flexible plates arranged like the teeth of a comb and frayed on the inner side to strain minute plankton from surrounding seawater. The first of these baleen whales, the gray whale, has no close relatives: it is the single species of the family Eschrichtidae.

The gray whale seems to be intermediate between a sleek rorqual and a stout right whale. It is moderately large in size, with a long, rigid snout and a double blowhole on top of its head in place of the single blowhole of a toothed whale. Instead of teeth, a line of short, yellowish baleen plates hangs like a fringe from the upper jaw. Two to four rudimentary furrows line the throat, in contrast to the smooth throat of a right whale and the deeply grooved throat of a rorqual. In place of a dorsal fin, the gray whale has a low hump on its back, followed by a series of small knobs running down to the flukes, an arrangement that resembles the large knobs which line the lower back of a sperm whale. The flippers are ovate with pointed tips; their shape is intermediate between the slender fins of a rorqual and the broad, square paddles of a right whale. Even the flukes repeat this divergence, by having a curiously serrated posterior border that resembles the serrated border on the flukes of a humpback.

Listed below is the gray whale with its common names, classification, and species.

GRAY WHALE

OTHER COMMON NAMES: Pacific gray whale, grayback whale, California gray whale, devil fish, hardhead, mussel digger
GENUS: *Eschrichtius*
SPECIES: gray whale, *Eschrichtius robustus,* the single species

Two male gray whales lifting a wounded female to the surface.

Gray Whale
Eschrichtius robustus

When a whale is seriously wounded or sick, it struggles to reach the surface, remaining there until weakness finally loosens its hold on life and it sinks into oblivion. In times of great peril, the gray whales, *Eschrichtius robustus,* respond to signs of distress by drawing close to assist an injured companion: it is also a time when males display a deep attachment and concern for females. One event on record tells of a female gray whale that was wounded and sinking rapidly until two males reached her side, lifted her to the surface and carefully kept her head above water until she recovered.

Among Eschrichtidae, males are smaller than females, growing to a length of 40 to 45 feet (12.2 to 14 meters), while females measure around 43 to 50 feet (13 to 15.2 meters), with a maximum weight of 73,000 pounds (33,000 kilograms). Roughened by extensive scarring, the head of a gray whale is usually encrusted with a beading of small barnacles and is noted for its very narrow snout, which curves gradually upward to a double blowhole. From this point, the line of a long, finless back continues until interrupted by a low hump, followed by eight to thirteen bumps on the caudal section. The flippers are broad and taper to a point, while the flukes are gracefully curved and pointed, with a serrated posterior margin. The upper jaw is lined on each side with 140 to 180 yellowish-white baleen plates which end in a fringe of coarse, thick bristles. Inside the mouth, there is a narrow, salmon-pink tongue tipped with pale gray, and on the lower throat there are two, three, or, rarely, four nonexpansive furrows 5 feet (1.5 meters) long. From snout to flukes, the slate-gray skin of the entire body is streaked and splotched by random scars and clusters of white barnacles.

Placid and shore-loving, gray whales are forced to spend most of their lives in travel. Sometime in March, solitary individuals or small groups composed of males, females, or mother whales with small calves leave the safety of shallow waters to begin their spring migration, an epic journey that starts in quiet lagoons on the coast of Baja California and proceeds northward through cold Pacific currents until they pass between the Aleutian Islands to reach the chill waters of the Bering, Beaufort and Chukchi seas late in May. There they pass the short months of summer feeding on enormous quantities

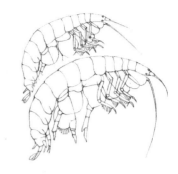

Gammaridean amphipods.

Northern anchovy and smelt.

Lateral and ventral views of baleen in the upper jaw.

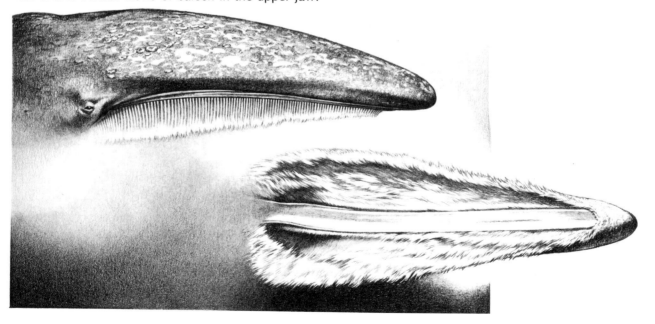

Gray whale mother and infant.

of plankton composed of amphipods and copepods, along with herring eggs and small schooling fish. When feeding, they sweep the ocean floor to gather a mouthful of bottom-dwelling amphipods and other marine organisms; then, rising vertically toward the surface, they sift all sand and silt from the food.

With the coming of October there is a change in loafing gray whales. Throughout their northern feeding grounds, they begin to turn southward in a movement that marks the beginning of the long return journey extending over 6,000 miles (9,600 kilometers) from the Bering, Chukchi, and Beaufort seas down to Baja California. Traveling at a speed of four to five knots, they round the Aleutians, move past distant Canadian shores, thread the forests of kelp along the coast of California, and arrive, in January, at Baja California.

In this barren desert land, the sea forms a maze of lagoons and quiet coves to provide a last refuge for the gray whales. It is also a nursery for their young. While some of the whales linger in the outer channels, those females close to delivery enter the lagoons and disperse to sheltered areas that have a shallow depth. In these quiet waters, the mother whale gives birth to a calf measuring 13 to 16 feet (4 to 5 meters) in length and weighing around 1,500 pounds (680 kilograms). Each infant enters the world after a gestation of thirteen months, its head sparsely covered with coarse, white hairs, its skin soft and black with a rubbery texture, and its body creased with fetal folds. The mother gray whale remains close to her calf and displays an unusual degree of affection, playing with the infant, supporting it on her back when it becomes tired, and keeping watch for any sign of an enemy. Sharks are a menace, as are the tides that ebb and flow, sometimes stranding the little whales on low sandbanks to die of exposure to the relentless heat of the sun and drying desert winds.

Each year, there is some infant mortality, but most of the young survive. The California gray whale is tough and resilient, rising from the brink of extinction in 1947 to a sound and stable population in recent years. Formerly found in Europe and Asia, they are now limited to the North Pacific from

Siberia and Alaska down to Mexico. Korean gray whales, once numerous in southeastern Asia, are now virtually extinct. Those whales that once roamed the Atlantic Ocean vanished centuries ago, leaving only a few fossil skeletons lying beneath the Zuider Zee and other areas to prove that *Eschrichtius robustus* once wandered close to the shores of Northern Europe.

The longest migration of any mammal is the 6,000-mile (9,600-kilometer) journey of the gray whale.

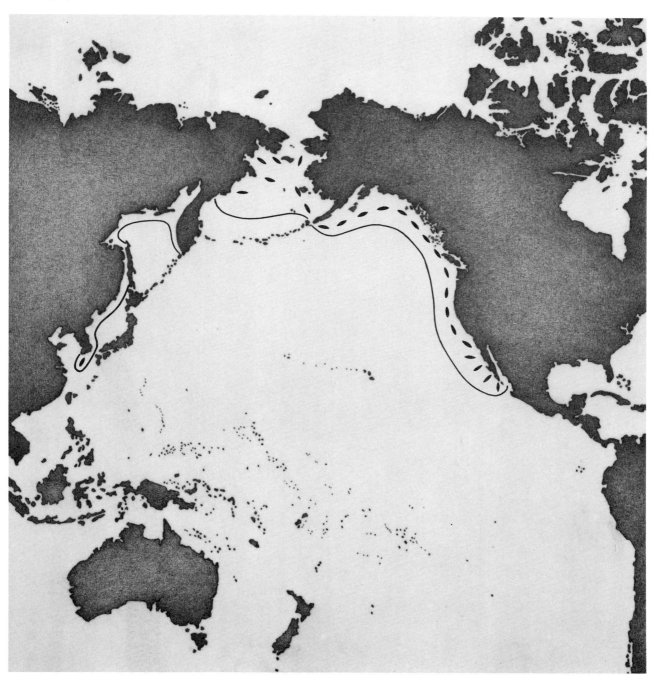

Balaenopterids: from top, fin whale, blue whale, and humpback.

Balaenopterids, Balaenopteridae

The family Balaenopteridae contains two famous genera, typified by the humpback and the rorquals (which include the blue whale, fin whale, sei whale, Bryde's whale, and the minke whale). The fame of the rorquals derives principally from the fact that these swift, slender whales grow to a considerable size and list among their members the great blue whale, the largest creature ever known to have lived on earth. This gentle leviathan was accorded the status of genus under the title *Sibbaldus musculus* until recent years, when it was reexamined, then placed among the rorquals and listed as *Balaenoptera musculus.*

The balaenopterids are seldom mistaken for other genera. In these whales, the body is usually lean and streamlined for speed, the head is shaped like a long, pointed wedge, and the lower surface of the throat and chest is lined with a large number of expandable grooves which extend from the lower lip to near the navel. In addition to these definitive characteristics, the baleen is composed of short, stiff plates; the flippers are very narrow and taper to a point; and the dorsal fin is moderate to very small and placed far down the back. It is interesting to note that, like the small river dolphins, the seven cervical vertebrae of these great whales are not fused; all of them move freely, although occasionally one or two may be partly fused.

Listed below are the balaenopterids, their common names, classifications, and numbers of species.

FIN WHALE
OTHER COMMON NAMES: finback, common rorqual, finner, razorback
GENUS: *Balaenoptera*
SPECIES: The genus *Balaenoptera* includes five species:
Fin whale, *Balaenoptera physalus*
Blue whale, *Balaenoptera musculus* (formerly *Sibbaldus musculus)*
Sei whale, *Balaenoptera borealis*
Bryde's whale, *Balaenoptera edeni*
Minke whale, *Balaenoptera acutorostrata*

HUMPBACK WHALE
OTHER COMMON NAMES: hump whale, hunchback whale
GENUS: *Megaptera*
SPECIES: humpback whale, *Megaptera novaeangliae,* the single species

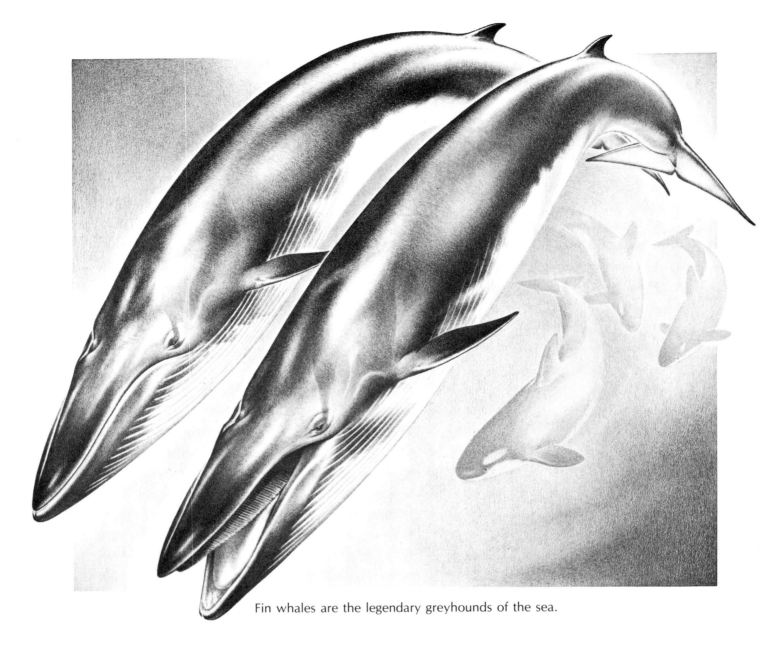

Fin whales are the legendary greyhounds of the sea.

Fin Whale
Balaenoptera physalus

Long, lean, and streamlined, the fin whales, *Balaenoptera physalus,* are the legendary "greyhounds of the sea." Shaped for great speed and endurance, these beautiful whales have V-shaped heads, tapering flippers, and broad, powerful flukes which propel their torpedo-like forms through surging water so swiftly that few predators can overtake them. When pursued by roving bands of killer whales, they can reach a speed of 25 miles per hour (41 kilometers per hour), maintaining this effort until the pulsing rhythm of the hunting pack no longer echoes close behind.

Fin whales, often called common rorquals, are very large baleen whales, with an average length of 65 to 70 feet (20 to 21 meters). Among those in the Antarctic region, however, some females may reach a maximum length of 82 feet (25 meters) and a weight ranging up to a maximum 80 tons (73,000 kilograms). The head of *B. physalus* is long and semiflat, shaped like a wedge and lined on the outside of both jaws with rows of tactile (or sensitive) hairs which end in a peculiar cluster at the tip of the lower jaw. Inside its mouth, there are 350 to 375 baleen plates, measuring around 36 inches (90 centimeters), suspended from each side of the upper jaw. From lower lip to past the navel, the throat of *B. physalus* is sectioned by fifty-six to a hundred long, deep furrows, or flexible grooves, which expand to increase the enormous storage capacity of the whale when feeding. Flippers are narrow and flukes have a triangular shape that is modified for speed. The long, tubular body is surmounted by a falcate dorsal fin placed far down on the curve of the back, with an extremely sharp dorsal ridge extending to the tail —a distinctive feature that has given *B. physalus* the name of "razorback."

Blending into the shadows of pelagic waters, fin whales are a dark bluish gray or brownish gray above, marked by pale chevrons, with the dark dorsal color fading on the sides in an irregular pattern to a pure, gleaming white on the undersurface of the body and the undersides of flippers and flukes. A yellow or green stain on the immaculate white skin of the abdomen is caused by a film of diatoms, or algae. In fin whales, the head varies in color, with the entire upper jaw, baleen, and left side of the lower jaw a very dark shade of blue-gray. On the right side, however, the lower jaw and front one third of the baleen are yellowish white in color and always identify *B. physalus*.

Although these whales are sometimes solitary, they customarily travel in groups ranging from a few individuals, up to assemblies of two or three hundred whales that wander through the deeper waters of all major oceans but seldom enter coastal zones. Their range includes the Greenland and Norwegian seas, the North Atlantic, North Pacific, and Arctic oceans. Fin whales are also found in the Indian Ocean, the South Atlantic and South Pacific oceans, and the more temperate areas of the Antarctic. While they do

Ivory white marks the right side of a fin whale's lower jaw and front section of baleen.

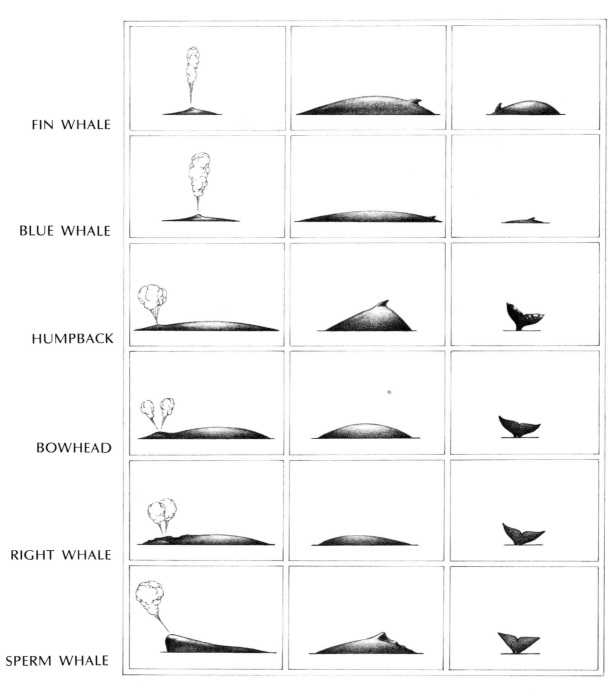

FIN WHALE

BLUE WHALE

HUMPBACK

BOWHEAD

RIGHT WHALE

SPERM WHALE

Blows and diving movements of large whales. (NOAA Technical Report NMFS CIRC-396.)

not penetrate as far into the ice fields of Antarctica as the blue whales, they do assemble near the outer perimeter of the continent to feast on clusters of finger-sized, shrimplike crustaceans.

Fin whales in the North Pacific search for schools of squid, tomcod, mackerel, and anchovies. In the North Atlantic, their diet consists of krill, capelin, herring, and other fish. Large fin whales in the Antarctic Ocean feed extensively on *Euphausia superba, E. vallentini,* and *Thysanoessa macrura,* the large proliferating krill that cloud the upper levels of Antarctic waters. When swallowed, the food of a rorqual is transferred consecutively to three gastric pouches, consisting of a forestomach which can hold 5 million krill weighing over 1 ton (900 kilograms), a main stomach, and a pyloric stomach. Since most whales swallow their food whole, without chewing, they must depend on stomach acids or heavy pleats lining the muscular walls of their forestomach to break food into very small portions. Often the forestomach will contain a number of stones weighing from a few ounces up to many pounds and a large or small amount of sand, all of these rotated by the walls of the stomach in a tumbling or pounding action, similar to that in the gizzard of a bird, which grinds krill and other food into a digestible consistency.

Among these swift and graceful whales, courtship takes place in winter, when the rorquals migrate to warm seas to breed. It is there that some of the females give birth to calves, measuring approximately 21 feet (6.5 meters) in length (twins occur infrequently). Within six months, each young whale has doubled its length to 39 feet (12 meters) and is weaned by the mother. Fully grown at around seven years, it can anticipate a long life, for recent studies have indicated that a fin whale may live from forty to one hundred years.

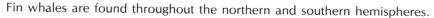

Fin whales are found throughout the northern and southern hemispheres.

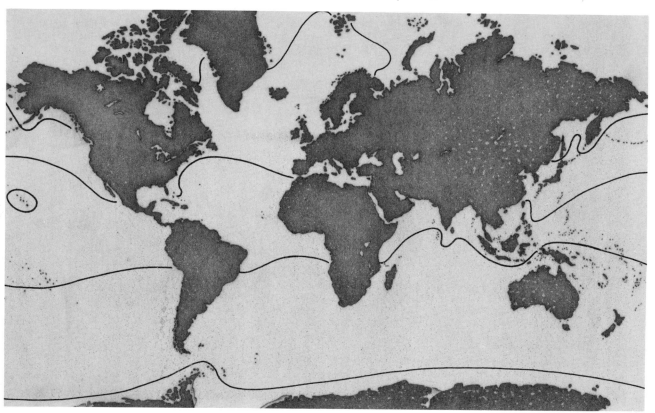

The great blue whale and young, accompanied by dolphins.

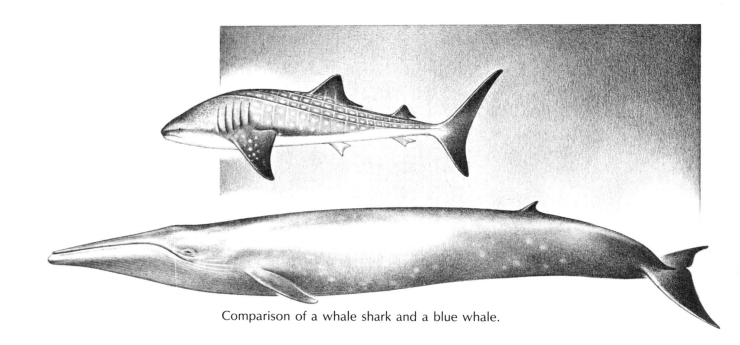

Comparison of a whale shark and a blue whale.

Blue Whale
Balaenoptera musculus

Gentle and shy in disposition, the great blue whale, *Balaenoptera musculus,* is believed to be the largest creature that has ever lived on earth, dwarfing even mighty *Brontosaurus,* the legendary thunder lizard of the Jurassic period. Two centuries ago, blue whales in the Antarctic reached an awesome length of 100 feet (30.5 meters) and weighed up to 150 tons (136,000 kilograms), a bulk equal to the combined weight of thirty elephants. Today, they are smaller, averaging 75 to 82 feet (23 to 25 meters) in length, with females slightly larger than males.

The head of the blue whale is long and U-shaped. Its upper jaw is flat with a prominent central ridge on top and a fringe of black baleen plates, numbering 270 to 395 in all, hanging from the inside rim of the upper jaw. Its throat and chest are lined with 55 to 120 pleated ventral grooves extending to the navel; the flippers, usually white on the tip and undersurface, are narrow and tapered, while its great flukes span a width of 15 to 20 feet (4.5 to 6 meters). The whale's long, sleek body is slate blue or bluish gray, sometimes mottled over the back, sides, and belly with clusters of pale gray spots, possibly the bite of the "cookie-cutter shark," *Isistius brasiliensis.*

Wandering alone or in very small groups during summer, blue whales haunt the edges of the polar pack ice in the Arctic and Antarctic, hunting for heavy concentrations of krill. On this inexhaustible abundance, the hungry whales grow fat, consuming from 1 to 4 tons (900 to 3,600 kilograms) of food per day until rapidly forming ice forces them to depart for the temperate waters of their breeding grounds.

Whales feeding in the Antarctic turn north toward South America, Australia, New Zealand, the coasts of South Africa, and the Indian Ocean. Those in the northern hemisphere, having fed on copepods and other crustaceans in the northern Pacific and Atlantic oceans turn south in winter to the warmth of North American and European waters. At the end of their journey, approximately eleven to twelve months after mating, many of the females give birth to calves measuring 23 to 25 feet (7 to 7.8 meters) in length and nurse their newborn young with an extremely concentrated milk that is yellow in color and contains 40 to 50 percent butterfat. On this exceedingly rich nourishment, an infant blue whale grows at the incredible rate of 200 pounds (90 kilograms) a day—or slightly under 4 tons (3,600 kilograms) in weight each month. Within twenty-three to thirty years the young whale reaches maturity at 75 feet (23 meters) and weighs around 70 tons (64,000 kilograms).

Now approaching extinction after centuries of slaughter, it is a matter of deep concern that these magnificent whales, intelligent and gentle in disposition, may become extinct in our time. The genus *Balaenoptera* contains five species: the fin whale, the blue whale (previously listed as *Sibbaldus musculus),* the sei whale, Bryde's whale, and the minke whale.

The range of blue whales is worldwide.

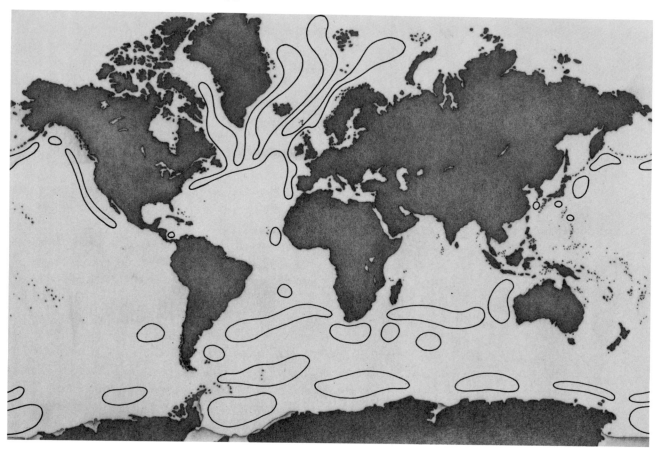

SPECIES OF *BALAENOPTERA*

Blue Whale, *Balaenoptera musculus.* In past centuries, this immense whale was reported to have reached an awesome length of 100 feet (30.5 meters) and a weight of 150 tons (136,000 kilograms). Bluish gray in color with black baleen, *B. musculus* occurs in most of the oceans.

Fin Whale, *Balaenoptera physalus.* Cosmopolitan in range, the fin whale measures approximately 63 to 82 feet (19 to 25 meters) in length. It is long and lean in shape with a sharp caudal ridge. The body is dark gray above and pure white below. Food consists of krill, fish, and squid.

Sei Whale, *Balaenoptera borealis.* These whales, sometimes called Rudolphi's rorquals, pollack whales, or sardine whales, are sleek and swift, with an average length of 48 feet (14.5 meters) for males, 51 feet (15.5 meters) for females, and a maximum length of 68 feet (21 meters). They are dark gray dorsally, fading to gray ventrally, with one area of grayish white on the chest. The 300 to 380 plates of black baleen are lined with fine, silken white bristles, and the long ventral grooves, thirty-eight to fifty-six in number, extend from the lower lip almost to the navel. Large herds of sei whales (pronounced "say") skim the surface for krill, copepods, squid, sardines, cod, herring, and sauries in temperate waters worldwide.

Bryde's Whale, *Balaenoptera edeni.* Moderate in size, with an average length of 43 feet (13 meters) for females and 40 feet (12 meters) for males, up to a maximum of 46 feet (14 meters), Bryde's whale (pronounced "breedah's") resembles the sei whale but has a longer body, with a shorter head, small, narrow flippers, and wide flukes. It should be noted that the sei whale has one central ridge on top of its head, while Bryde's whale has three ridges. There are forty-five throat furrows extending to the navel, and the baleen, short and pale gray in front, darkens to grayish black in back. Color is usually limited to dark blue-gray above and lighter below. *B. edeni* feeds on krill and dives deep in search of squid, crustaceans, anchovy, sardines, herring, mackerel, and sand lance. Often solitary, Bryde's whales are found in tropical and subtropical seas between 40° north and 40° south latitudes.

Minke Whale, *Balaenoptera acutorostrata.* Called little piked whale, lesser rorqual, and little finner, this smallest member of the rorquals reaches a length of 26 to 30 feet (8 to 9 meters) and a weight of around 10 tons (9,000 kilograms). Slender in form, it has a short, sharply pointed head, a high, falcate dorsal fin, moderately broad flukes, and fifty to seventy ventral grooves. Minke whales are black or blue-gray above and pure white below, shading to gray on the lower caudal section. A distinctive white band (sometimes absent in southern whales) crosses each flipper. The baleen plates, numbering 280 to 325 per side, are composed of short, yellowish-white to brown bristles of fine texture. Worldwide in distribution, minke whales (pronounced "minkeh") advance into the pack ice of Arctic and Antarctic seas.

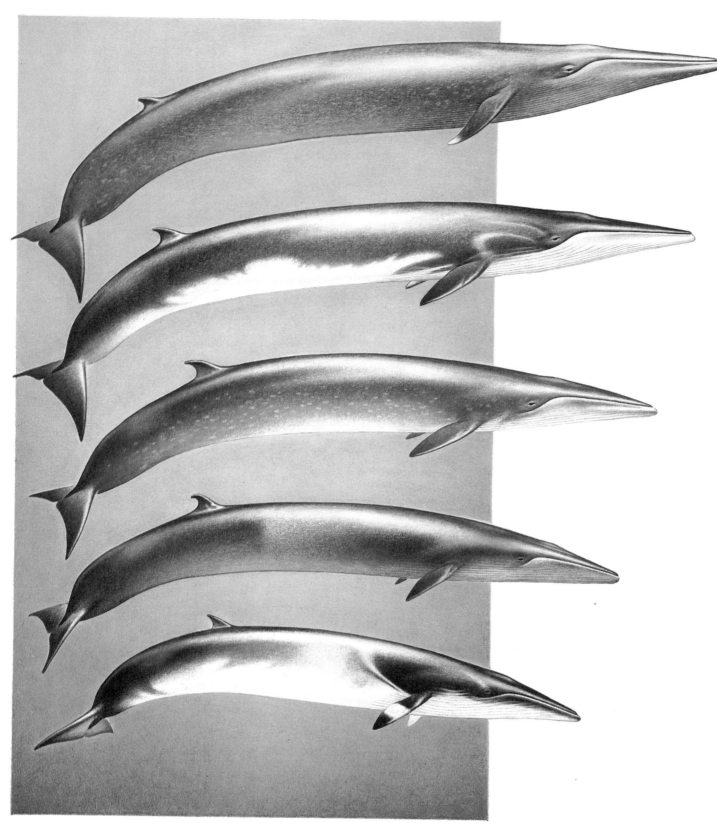

Species of *Balaenoptera:* blue whale, *B. musculus;* fin whale, *B. physalus;* sei whale, *B. borealis;* Bryde's whale, *B. edeni;* minke whale, *B. acutorostrata.*

The magnificent breaching of a humpback whale.

Humpback Whale
Megaptera novaeangliae

The breaching of a humpback whale is a magnificent display of power. Beginning far down in blue-green depths as a rising blur of movement, it ends with an explosive eruption out of a calm sea in a violent surge of action that hurls over fifty tons of massive bone and muscle soaring up and up in a towering leap, circled by swirling waters and veils of flying spray.

In contrast to a sleek and shapely fin whale, the humpback, *Megaptera novaeangliae,* is stocky and powerful, ranging from 40 feet (12 meters) up to a rare maximum of 62 feet (19 meters) in length, with an average weight of over thirty tons. The whale's head is large and moderately flat, embossed on top by uneven rows of fleshy knobs, and lined inside the mouth with 270 to 400 short plates of ash or olive-black baleen suspended from each side of the upper jaw. Placed well past the midpoint of the whale's back, a small dorsal fin varies in contour from sharply falcate to an irregular humped triangle rising above a slender caudal section which tapers rapidly down to enormous flukes that are deeply notched and have a serrated rear border. On the underside, from lower jaw to navel, the abdomen is furrowed by the folds of fourteen to twenty-four long grooves, much deeper and wider than those of a fin whale. Colonies of barnacles thrive on the surfaces of these flexible folds, attaching their round shells to the pleated throat, flippers, or flukes, accumulating in such large numbers that a whale eventually may carry half a ton of tiny limestone shells.

A humpback is black, with individual variation in the amount of white spotting on the underside. Some northern whales are entirely black, while others show a more common mottled streaking or a brilliant white throat and breast, with the black color on the upper surface of flippers and flukes often extending onto the white underside.

Inside the body of this whale there are one or two small bones buried deep beneath the muscles of the lower side. These vestigial bits of bone are all that remain, after millions of years, of the whale's pelvis and the femur of a hind leg. In July of 1919, an event of some importance occurred when the body of a female humpback was brought aboard a whaling ship out of Vancouver Island, British Columbia. Unaware of any unusual circumstance, the ship's crew removed an abnormal growth extending from the lower side of the whale. A similar growth attached to the opposite side of the body was also removed, but instead of being discarded, fortunately was obtained by Mr. Francis Kermode, Director of the Provincial Museum, and sent to Professor Roy Chapman Andrews, of the American Museum of Natural History. A résumé of his report follows.

The female humpback was found to have a primitive leg, which extended outside the body to a length of 4 feet (1.3 meters). Within this shaftlike mass of tissue, there were two bones and also two sections of cartilage which were

Rising out of
blue-green depths.

Ventral and dorsal views of a humpback.

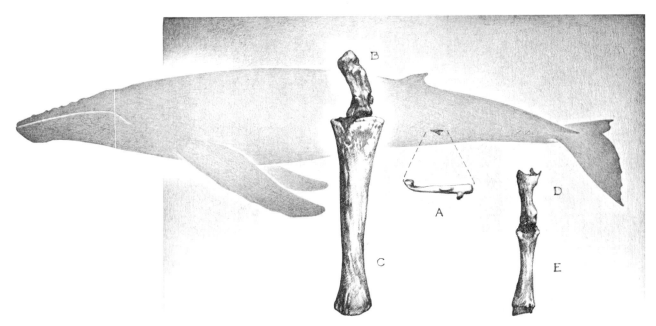

A very rare example of regression to a four-legged condition in a humpback.

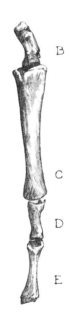

apparently reduced to a fraction of their former size by shrinkage. Andrews hypothesized that in life the sequence of articulation in the leg began with a vestigial pelvis (A), then the femoral cartilage (B), followed by the tibia (C), the tarsal cartilage (D), and ended with the metatarsal bone (E): tarsus represents the ankle region and metatarsus represents the foot minus its toes. In estimating the original measurements before shrinkage occurred, Andrews listed the femoral cartilage at 15 inches (380 millimeters) long by 3 inches (76 millimeters) wide; attached to the tibia (bone) with a length of 14 by 3.7 inches (362 by 95 millimeters) wide proximally and 2.5 inches (64 millimeters) wide distally; followed by the tarsal cartilage, measuring 15 inches (380 millimeters); then the metatarsal bone, 6 inches (155 millimeters) in length, which formed the end of a primitive leg. Mr. Andrews concluded that the specimen represented a clear case of the partial reversion of a whale to a four-legged condition.

It is the flippers of *Megaptera,* however, that command attention. These armlike appendages are unique among whales. Reaching a size equal to one third of the total body length and resembling flexible clubs, they possess enough raw force to fracture the bones of marauding killer whales. Indeed, when surrounded by a pack of leaping orcas, a humpback will rise on the surface and lash the darting black-and-white forms by striking out with long, powerful flippers, landing blows that descend with crushing impact. Perhaps this willingness to fight for life is the reason killer whales do not always succeed when challenging a fighter like *Megaptera.*

Humpbacks are a coast-loving species, fond of exploring inshore areas and sometimes stranding in unfamiliar waters. These inquisitive whales have a habit of wandering in a leisurely, erratic way, often accompanied by playful groups of bottlenose dolphins, pilot whales, spinner dolphins or, occasionally, a large procession of pygmy killer whales.

Migrating along established routes, many humpbacks spend their summers in the cold, invigorating currents of the Arctic or Antarctic ocean. They enter ice-free bays and coastal areas as the lengthening days of summer transform surface waters into a lush pasture of microscopic plants surrounded by dense clouds of zooplankton composed primarily of copepods or krill feeding on the tiny green plants. To collect this swarm of tiny creatures, the humpback cruises at a twilight depth of around 65 feet (20 meters) and comes to a pause as a mass of krill darkens the water overhead. Drifting upward, the whale begins to ascend in a slow spiral, releasing a stream of bubbles that rises like a circular curtain of shimmering white mist, surrounding and concentrating the frightened krill into a large bite-sized lump. In this manner, the humpback traps its prey, but it is not limited to one technique. The long flippers can sweep krill into its gaping mouth, or the great flukes can fling water ahead of the whale to confuse the krill until a pair of wide jaws close over them. When copepods and other crustaceans are in short supply, schools of capelin, anchovy, and other small fish are followed by the adaptable humpback.

The preference of baleen whales for krill and other small crustaceans has caused profound changes in some of their internal organs. Their problem centers on the salinity of seawater, which is so high in salt content (at 3.5 percent) that mammals, including the whales, dolphins, and porpoises, are unable to swallow large amounts of it. Many of the marine mammals, particularly the toothed whales, seals, sea lions, and otters, manage to avoid any danger by obtaining adequate fresh water from the fish they consume: the baleen whales are not so fortunate.

Humpbacks and other baleen whales devour enormous quantities of invertebrates such as copepods, euphausiids, amphipods, and other small crustaceans. Unfortunately, all of these tiny creatures have a saline content equal

Mother and twins.

201

to the seawater in which they live, and with each great mouthful of food, the whales also swallow a copious amount of salt. Cetologists have theorized that large reserves of water must be withdrawn from their blood, intestines, and blubber in order to rid their bodies of this toxic substance and flush the heavy concentrations of salt out of their systems. The filtering organs, or kidneys, of baleen whales are noticeably enlarged and contain an extraordinary number of lobes, or renculi (small filtering units resembling tiny kidneys) that cluster in hundreds or thousands to form a pair of long, rather flat organs that filter out salt and other toxic chemicals before returning (in theory) a part of the now purified water to the whale's system. It is possible this same procedure is followed by the beaked whales and a number of dolphins and porpoises that prefer squid, another invertebrate with a very high salt content.

In late summer, the whales begin a long, leisurely journey toward their winter range. Immature males and mother whales with young are the first to depart, then large groups of adult males and females, followed by young males and females. Ultimately, their journey will end in the warm oceans near Bermuda, the Hawaiian Islands, and other tropical climates worldwide. It is in these clear, sunlit waters that the high emotions of the courting season reach a climax among incoming groups.

As the number of arriving whales increases, adult males become more aggressive and begin to skirmish for position, each one seeking to accompany a female and showing truculence when a rival ventures too close. The male escort may blow a stream of bubbles as a mild warning, or, if angered, he will charge a persistent opponent, smashing into the other whale with considerable force in a persuasive action which could end the contest at once; or the two may battle with jaws, flippers, and lashing flukes until one of the combatants breaks away and retreats to try his luck elsewhere.

For some of the females, the long migration to their winter range marks the end of a gestation period of approximately eleven months, when each one gives birth to a single calf, or rarely twins, measuring 13 to 14 feet (4 to 4.5 meters) in length. The little whale will be nursed for seven months and will remain close to its mother, taking refuge under her body when frightened and resting on her back when tired.

The female spreads her great flippers and glides forward in a languorous, dreamlike state.

Among courting whales, the selection of a partner proceeds at a varied pace, with many roaming through the depths, while others rest on the surface. In a playful frame of mind, a male will chase a coquettish female, striking the object of his interest with long flippers in a series of love pats that can be heard far over the water; or, in a tender mood, he will stroke the female with lingering touches that express a sensitive gentleness, and the female eventually may respond by spreading her great flippers and gliding through the water with indescribable grace in a languorous, dreamlike state, accompanied by her attentive suitor.

It is a time of emotional outpouring among the whales, not only in birth, courtship, and battle, but also, surprisingly, in song. To express this inner compulsion, a whale quietly withdraws to a secluded area below the surface and rests motionless in the dim twilight, eyes closed, body suspended at a 45° angle with drooping head and limp flippers. The blowhole is tightly closed, releasing no bubbles; however, from this solitary whale a haunting melody pours forth, full of eerie notes and an extensive range of sounds that resemble distant thunder, a creaking door, tremulous cries and moans, or a series of sharply rising "wheeps." The song is incredibly beautiful in its strangeness, like music from a distant sphere.

Humpbacks are worldwide in distribution. Those in the northern hemisphere travel a vast circuit from just north of the equator to a point 70° north, and those in the southern hemisphere, now severely depleted in numbers, follow a similar circuit from just south of the equator into the pack ice of the Antarctic. Few whales command more interest or more affection than the gentle giant called the humpback.

Humpback whales are found in all the great oceans.

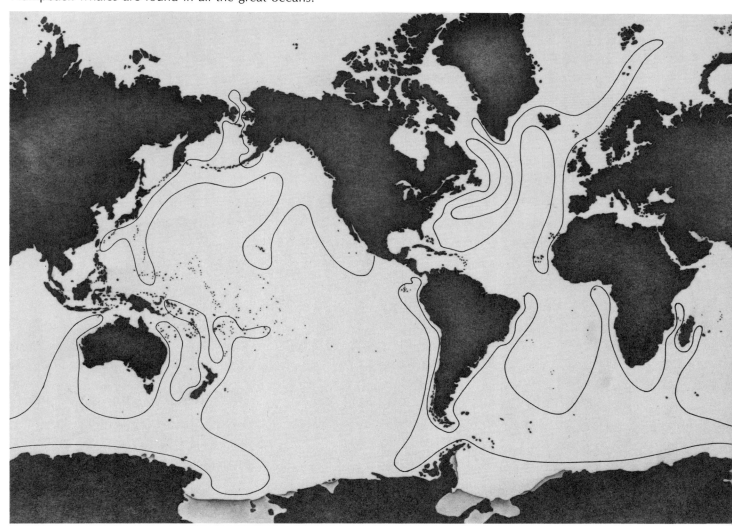

Right whales: from top, bowhead, right whale, and pygmy right whale.

Right Whales, Balaenidae

The family Balaenidae contains two very rare and remarkable whales whose tragic history is well known: the bowhead and the right whale. Also included in the family is a rather obscure little relative from the southern hemisphere called the pygmy right whale. These three balaenids, slow in movement and placid in temperament, can be identified by several unusual characteristics, which consist of a narrow, highly arched upper jaw and a broad, enveloping lower lip; a smooth throat and chest, without deep furrows or grooves; and seven cervical vertebrae which have been fused into a solid mass of bone.

In this group, the bowhead and the right whale share certain unique features. Each has an enormous head; extremely long, flexible baleen plates which may extend over 10 feet (3 meters) in length; a smooth back with no trace of a dorsal fin; large, squared flippers; gracefully tapered flukes; and a very robust form. The small pygmy right whale superficially resembles the rorquals, since it has a small dorsal fin and slender flippers, but its mouth is bowed in the high arch of the right whales, and its cervical vertebrae are completely fused.

Listed below are the three right whales, their common names, classifications, and species.

BOWHEAD
OTHER COMMON NAMES: Greenland right whale, great polar whale
GENUS: *Balaena*
SPECIES: bowhead, *Balaena mysticetus,* the single species

RIGHT WHALE
OTHER COMMON NAMES: black right whale, Biscayan right whale, North Atlantic right whale
GENUS: *Eubalaena*
SPECIES: right whale, *Eubalaena glacialis,* the single species

PYGMY RIGHT WHALE
OTHER COMMON NAME: none
GENUS: *Caperea*
SPECIES: pygmy right whale, *Caperea marginata,* the single species

The bowhead whale.

Bowhead
Balaena mysticetus

Looming dark against a wall of emerald-tinted ice, the bowhead, *Balaena mysticetus,* is a very impressive whale. Its massive head, measuring one third of total body length, is divided by a cavernous mouth equipped with a bowed upper jaw and heavy lower jaw, which can form an opening large enough to engulf a young elephant: the throat that opens behind these jaws, however, is exceedingly small, measuring a mere 4.3 inches (11 centimeters) in diameter.

The bowhead is also noted for the absence of a dorsal fin. Its back curves in a long, smooth line from neck to flukes without a break in the flat surface, a feature that allows the whale to ram heavy ice formations from below in order to break open a breathing hole. Its body is unusually robust in form, expanding to a wide girth immediately behind the flippers, then tapering rapidly down to broad flukes. Maximum length for adults has been established at approximately 50 to 58 feet (15 to 18 meters). Its flippers are large, appearing more squared and handlike than the streamlined forms of rorquals, while its flukes, broad and powerful, have a magnificent spread of 18 feet (5.5 meters).

The whale is velvet black, enhanced by a large "vest" of cream or ash white on its lower jaw which covers the chin and may extend along its lower lip. Stretching from the tip of the lower jaw back across the white vest, there is a row of irregular spots that resembles a string of large black beads and serves as an identifying mark for bowheads. Scoresby (1820) added to our knowledge of this nearly extinct whale by describing in detail its shape, color, and habits, reporting that the tip of the upper jaw and part of the baleen may be white with grayish areas appearing on the eyelids and around the insertion of flippers and the juncture of the flukes and body. He observed some whales that were completely piebald and described nursing young as gray-blue in color, while old individuals, hoary with years, were reported as displaying considerable gray or white.

Bowheads are confined to the Arctic Ocean and adjacent areas, with their migratory movements governed by seasonal changes in the polar pack ice. Sometime in May or June, when the ice begins to break up and melt, a small number of whales in the Bering Sea leave the open waters of their winter range and move northward. All of these whales, including young calves swimming close to their mother's side, follow the swift Bering Current through the narrow opening of Bering Strait in June and proceed to the Beaufort Sea, the Mackenzie River, and scattered northern islands. In these sheltered areas, they feed on swarms of copepods, the "krill" of northern latitudes.

Being leisurely creatures, bowheads rest on the surface for half an hour, then submerge for ten to twenty minutes. Cruising open-mouthed through heavy concentrations of copepods and other tiny living organisms that cloud the upper levels, each whale dives and closes its jaws, forcing all seawater out through a screen of 325 to 360 long, blackish-gray baleen plates measuring up to 13 feet (4 meters) in length.

The whales linger in Arctic waters until winter's first storms appear in September. As the grip of cold intensifies, the temperature of seawater around the whales, chilled by frigid winds, gradually begins to fall until it reaches 28°. At this point, the first delicate films of sea ice appear on the surface, constantly shattering under the impact of waves and re-forming, eventually thickening into a glistening sheet as lower levels are frozen, until the whales are no longer able to break its surface easily for breathing, and are forced to begin their retreat to the south. Moving ahead of an advancing ice sheet, they pass through Bering Strait into the safety of the Bering Sea and seek refuge in open waters above the Aleutian and Kuril islands.

Dorsal view of a female bowhead and young.

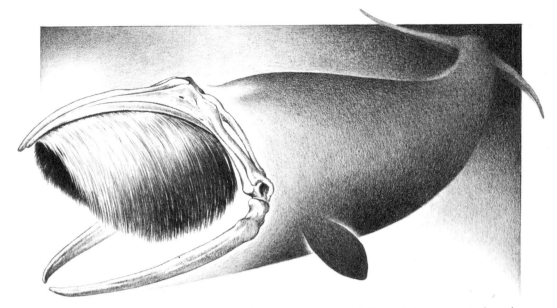

The luxuriant baleen of a bowhead measures up to 14 feet (4.3 meters) in length.

Copepods.

In fog-shrouded coastal waters and the sheltered bays of their winter range, sometime in February or March, many of the females give birth to a single calf measuring approximately 10 to 18 feet (3 to 5.4 meters). Throughout the following twelve months, the mother shows a great deal of concern for her infant and will sacrifice her life for its safety. Scoresby commented on the common practice among whaling crews of securing a small bowhead, then attempting to kill the mother whale when she surfaced. And she would return in an effort to free the little whale by touching it, testing the harpoon or rope, and on one occasion, even wrecking the crew's longboat with her great flukes. Scoresby listed one encounter in which the mother was struck by six harpoons and remained with her wounded young. It is estimated that this genocidal method of securing both the young and mother whale eventually destroyed great populations. At this time, a few living bowhead whales have been reported from the Siberian, Bering, Okhotsk, Chukchi, Beaufort and Greenland seas, with confirmed observations from Hudson's Bay, Davis Strait, and the coasts of Alaska.

The survival of these unique whales is in doubt. Although protected by a belated international agreement, they are scattered over vast areas and their numbers do not increase easily. Most of those left alive are confined to the Alaskan and Canadian Arctic. Before the seventeenth century, immense numbers of bowhead whales were found throughout the Arctic regions of Eurasia and North America, ranging from eastern Siberia to Spitsbergen, Greenland, and down to Newfoundland. Today, nearly exterminated by the slaughter of whaling fleets for over three hundred years, the remnants of these once magnificent herds have shrunk to small groups or solitary whales that cling to the shelter of ice floes in remote areas of the Arctic Ocean and adjacent seas. They are almost extinct.

Bowhead whales are confined to arctic regions.

Two great right whales dive deep in the chill waters near Iceland.

Right Whale
Eubalaena glacialis

In a windswept sea near Iceland, two black whales dive down, sending a shower of bright bubbles streaming upward from their smooth sides as they glide lower, descending through sunlit surface water into a nebulous, blue-green gloom that deepens to indigo darkness far below them. In this stormy region, currents are strong and the sea is chilled by glacial waters surging down from the Arctic Ocean.

Scarcely .3 inch (7 millimeters) thick, the skin of the right whale, *Eubalaena glacialis,* appears to be a very frail guard against frigid arctic temperatures, but the whale does not feel the cold. Beneath this thin covering of skin, there is a deep layer of fat that wraps the whale's body in warm comfort even when immersed in ice-laden northern waters. This insulating fat, or blubber, is remarkably heavy on right whales and bowheads, ranging in thickness from 15.7 inches (400 millimeters) up to a maximum 28 inches (710 millimeters) in some parts. The entire layer of blubber actually represents 30 to 45 percent of the whale's total weight.

In body structure, the bowhead and the right whale are similar. The right whale is noted for its large head, the absence of a dorsal fin on its flat back, extremely long baleen, a smooth throat without furrows, and a massive black body with a girth that is often equal to its length, around 50 feet (15 meters) for an average whale. Its flippers are large, with a semisquared lower edge, and its short caudal section ends in broad flukes which curve out to a pointed tip, then curve back into a deep center notch. The spread of these enormous flukes is equal to 35 percent of the whale's length. Its back is dark and is usually called black, but a close examination often will reveal a deep brown or mottled blackish-brown tint that contrasts sharply with the random white splotches that sometimes cover its abdomen.

Skull and baleen of a right whale.

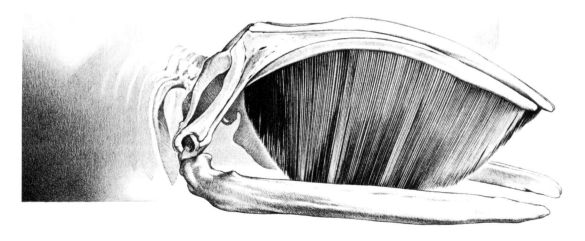

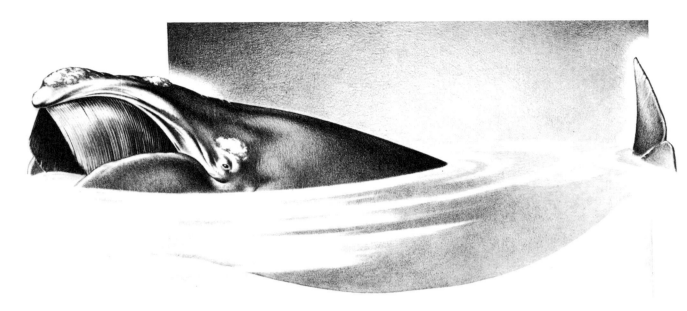

Right whale feeding on crustaceans.

The identifying mark of the right whale is a series of raised, ivory-white patches composed of callused layers of skin that dot the top and sides of the head and provide a haven for colonies of barnacles and other parasites. The largest mound, or "bonnet," is placed near the front of the whale's upper jaw, followed by other callused areas situated above the eyes and scattered along the upper and lower jaws in individual patterns. Two slit-like nostrils converge to form a V on top of its head, and inside the whale's mouth, suspended from both sides of the narrow, highly arched upper jaw, there are approximately 250 long, limber plates of dark, olive-gray baleen that sweep downward, with the frayed inner edges of the plates interlacing to form a dense webbing that traps small marine organisms.

To nourish their vast bulk, right whales feast on copepods and other crustaceans forming a part of the minute plankton drifting near the surface in heavy concentrations. In order to gather this abundant supply, the whale opens its mouth with the upper jaw held above the surface as it moves forward, then closes the broad lower jaw while its thick, blue-gray tongue presses water out through an interwoven screen formed by the long, fringed baleen blades.

These are shore-loving whales, preferring shallow waters bordering remote islands and the coastlines of uninhabited land areas. Amiable and placid, they usually proceed at a slow pace, averaging about 2.3 miles per hour (2 knots). When diving, southern whales remain submerged for a very short time (around two to three minutes), then surface for eight to nine minutes. They like to float in calm waters after feeding, and drowse in warm sunlight. In a playful mood, however, one will heave its ponderous bulk high above the surface, then come crashing down in a torrent of white spray, much as other great whales do; but right whales also use the surface wind currents as no other whale does.

Among marine life, the Portuguese man-of-war and the great right whale "sail" before the wind. To accomplish this feat, a submerged whale lifts its tail above the surface, adjusts its immense flukes at an angle to the wind, and moves out before a stiff breeze to cruise in a leisurely manner (Roger Payne, personal observation). This same strategy, with a few variations, is used by a reluctant female to avoid mating. She will lift the rear part of her body above the surface, remaining in this position as long as an amorous male waits below, or until she relents and accepts his attentions.

After a period of twelve months, as the time of delivery draws near, the female retires to a quiet area, where she gives birth to a single infant approximately 16 to 20 feet (5 to 6 meters) long. The little whale is grayish blue when first born, gradually changing, as it reaches maturity, to a deep brown or black color at times mottled with white spots on the abdomen or, on rare occasions, displaying a pure white belly. The young whale remains with its mother for more than a year, and the attachment between them is very strong. According to reports, a right-whale mother is very protective of her young. In the early days of whaling, the Bay of Biscay, lying off the northern coast of Spain, was one of the first hunting areas for right whales. Beddard (1900), p. 137, recorded one incident in which a small calf was harpooned by villagers. Instead of fleeing from danger, the mother whale hovered near her injured young, trying to pull it free of the harpoon until she finally broke the line and, taking the little whale in her flippers, carried it away into the depths of the bay.

From the twelfth century to the present, the gentle right whales were drastically reduced in numbers by a developing whaling industry which proceeded to slaughter entire populations so efficiently that by the nineteenth century, all of the immense herds in the northern and southern hemispheres were virtually annihilated. Very rare now in all areas, a few survivors from those vanished herds are still being found alive in remote parts of the Atlantic, Pacific and Indian oceans.

Mother whale removing her infant from danger.

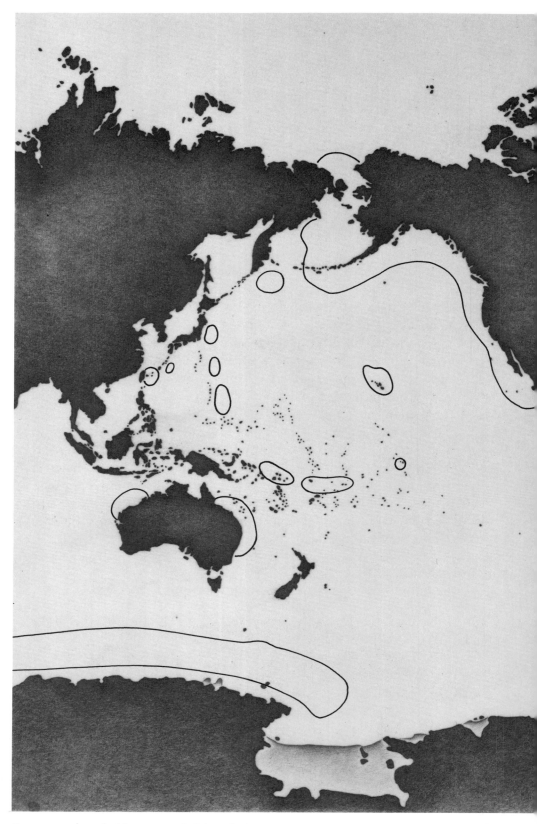

Known and probable range of right whales.

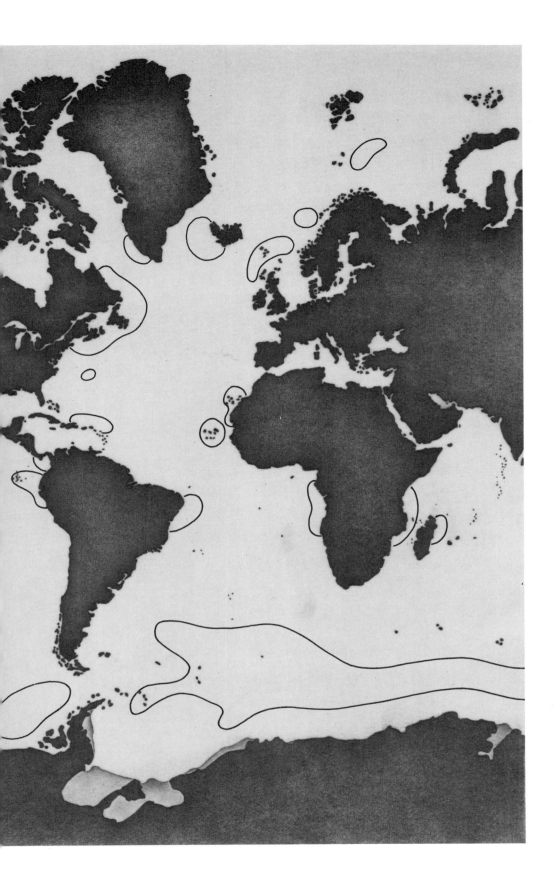

The pygmy right whale, smallest of the baleen whales.

Pygmy Right Whale
Caperea marginata

The internal structure of the pygmy right whale, *Caperea marginata*, is remarkable. Inside the body of this small whale there are seventeen pairs of ribs branching out from a long spine, with each pair of ribs becoming wider and longer as they approach the midpoint of the body. The continuation of these enveloping ribs (no other whale has so many) along the spine is so extensive that only two free vertebrae lie between those vertebrae which are connected with the ribs and the few remaining ones forming a short tail section. The entire skeleton resembles a cage-like enclosure assembled to provide unusual protection for the whale's internal organs.

Closely related to the great bowhead and right whales, the pygmy right whale is the smallest member of the Mysticeti, or baleen whales, reaching an average length of 21 feet (6.3 meters), with its head measuring approximately one fourth of body length. Instead of a smooth, finless back like its large relatives, the little whale has a small falcate dorsal fin, similar to that of a rorqual; its flippers are short and rather slender with a semiround tip, and its flukes are wide with a definite median notch. One interesting feature is the presence of two shallow indentations, or grooves, separated by three short, distinct ridges on each side of the lower throat, which form a curved profile for its lower jaw.

Color is limited to slate gray or black on the back, sides, flippers, and flukes, changing to silvery white or gray below. Records of pale gray immature individuals suggest that a darker gray color may come with advancing age. In sharp contrast to the dark color of its head, the whale's mouth and tongue are white, with a peculiar fringe edging the tip of the tongue; and its baleen, composed of 230 rather short plates on each side of the upper jaw, is a glistening ivory white with dark outer edges. Recently it was discovered that the gum line above the baleen of *Caperea* is pure white and often flashes in the sunlight when the whale surfaces.

Although little is known of *Caperea's* habits, it has been established that the small whale follows and feeds on drifting colonies of zooplankton, particularly copepods of the *Calanus* species, which form a part of the mysterious DSL, or deep scattering layer, in the middle depths. These small crustaceans are translucent and resemble long grains of rice equipped with sweeping antennae and tail. They form a very important part of marine ecology, because copepods consume enormous quantities of floating algae, only to be eaten, in turn, by larger krill, fish, and the great baleen whales. But the most astounding discovery about these tiny crustaceans is the vertical migration they make every day between the depths and upper levels of the ocean.

The extension of ribs in *C. marginata* is remarkable.

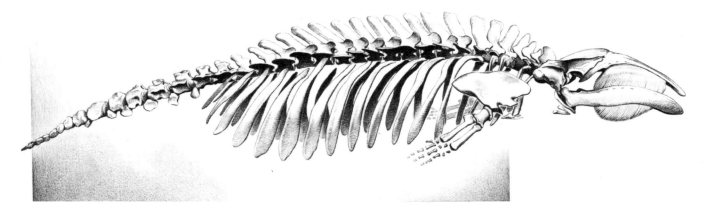

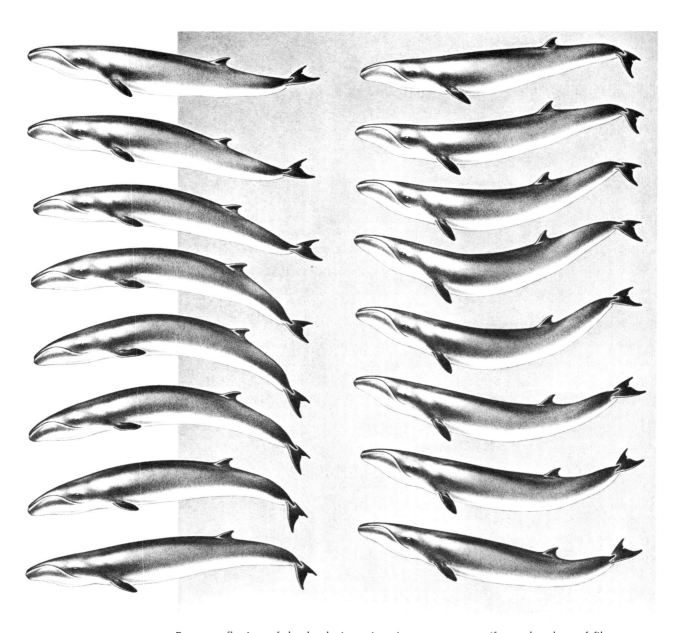

Extreme flexing of the body in swimming movements (from sketches of films made by Mr. T. Dicks).

At dusk, copepods leave their daytime resting places in the shadowy depths of 950 to 1,500 feet (290 to 450 meters) and slowly, with vigorous effort for such frail and fairy-like creatures, ascend at a speed of 150 feet (45 meters) per hour to the top level of the ocean to feed on concentrations of algae floating close to the surface; then, near dawn, they descend once more to the depths at a pace three times faster than their ascent. Pygmy right whales search the surface waters for large masses of these tiny copepods and other crustaceans.

Records indicate that the season of breeding and birth for these rare whales may extend over a considerable period of time. Although no measurements have been made of newborn infants, an estimate based on 26 to 33 percent of the mother whale's length (among balaenids) would produce a theoretical length of 5 to 7 feet (1.5 to 2.2 meters) for a newborn pygmy right whale. It has been suggested that some of the smaller whales moving through coastal waters in spring and early summer near southern Australia and New Zealand probably are wandering juveniles that have dispersed after weaning.

In December of 1967, a living pygmy right whale was sighted in Plettenberg Bay, at the tip of South Africa. Taking advantage of an unusual opportunity to record the appearance and behavior of this relatively unknown species, Mr. T. Dicks managed to produce an underwater film documenting the action of its body in fast and slow motion from many angles. In swimming, there was extensive flexing of the entire body with flippers held close in fast movement but relaxed when the pace was more moderate. Swimming speed, estimated at around 3.6 miles per hour (3.2 knots) was unexpectedly slow. This may hamper the small whales, because they have been known to accompany groups of dolphins or a large sei whale and her calf, and on one occasion, a single female pygmy right whale was sighted in the middle of a migrating band of pilot whales.

Limited to the southern hemisphere, this rare little whale has been recorded near New Zealand (thirteen sightings), Tasmania (fourteen), Western Australia (one), South Australia, (three), South Africa (nine), and the Crozet Islands region, in the southeastern Indian Ocean (one).

Limited range of pygmy right whales.

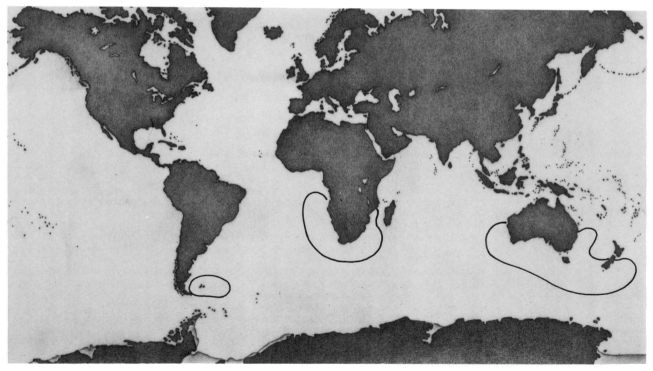

Bibliography

A Guide Book to South African Whales and Dolphins. South African Museum, Cape Town, South Africa. Guide No. 4, 1954.

AGUAYO L., A. "Progress Report of Small Cetacean Research in Chile," *Journal of the Fisheries Research Board of Canada,* Vol. 32 (1975) (7): 1123–43.

ALLEN, GLOVER M. "Burmeister's Porpoise *(Phocoena Spinipinnis),*" *Bulletin of the Museum of Comparative Zoology at Harvard College,* Vol. LXVII (1925), no. 5, pp. 251–59, 3 pls.

———. "Sowerby's Whale on the American Coast," *Amer. Nat.,* Vol. 30 (1906), no. 473, 4 figs., pp. 357–70.

———. "The Whalebone Whales of New England," *Memoirs of the Boston Society of Natural History,* Vol. 8 (1916), no. 2, pp. 108–322, illus.

ANDREWS, ROY C. "American Museum Whale Collection," *Amer. Mus. Jour.,* Vol. 14 (1914), no. 8, pp. 275–94, illus.

ASH, C. *Whaler's Eye.* New York: The Macmillan Company, 1962.

BEDDARD, F. E. *A Book of Whales.* New York: G. P. Putnam's Sons, 1900.

BERRILL, N. J., in collaboration with World Book Encyclopedia. *The Life of the Ocean.* New York: McGraw-Hill, 1966.

BOSCHMA, H. "Maxillary teeth in specimens of *Hyperoodon rostratus* (Müller) and *Mesoplodon grayi* (von Haast) stranded on the Dutch Coasts," *Proc. Koninklijke Nederlandse Akademie Van Wetenschappen,* Vol. LIII (1950), no. 6, pp. 775–85.

BRIMLEY, H. H. "*Kogia breviceps* and *Mesoplodon mirus* in the Neighborhood of the Oregon Inlet, North Carolina." *Journal of Mammalogy,* Vol. 26 (1946), no. 4, p. 434.

BROWN, D. H., and K. S. NORRIS. "Observations of Captive and Wild Cetaceans," *Journal of Mammalogy,* 37 (1956) (3), pp. 311–26, illus.

BROWNELL, R. L., JR. "Progress Report on the Biology of the Franciscana Dolphin, *Pontoporia blainvillei,* in Uruguayan Waters," *Journal of the Fisheries Research Bureau of Canada,* Vol. 32 (1975) (7): 1073–78.

——— and EARL S. HERALD. "*Lipotes vexillifer,*" *Am. Soc. Mammalian Species,* no. 10 (1972), pp. 1–4, 4 figs.

BUCHSBAUM, R., and LORUS J. MILNE. *The Lower Animals: Living Invertebrates of the World.* New York: Doubleday & Company, n.d.

CALDWELL, DAVID K., MELBA C. CALDWELL, and DALE C. RICE. "Behavior of the Sperm Whale, *Physeter catodon* L.," in *Whales, Dolphins, and Porpoises,* ed. K. S. Norris. Berkeley and Los Angeles: University of California Press, 1966, p. 677–718.

CALDWELL, MELBA C., and DAVID K. CALDWELL. "Epimeletic (Care-giving) Behavior in Cetacea," in *Whales, Dolphins, and Porpoises,* ed. K. S. Norris. Berkeley and Los Angeles: University of California Press, 1966, pp. 755–89.

CALDWELL, MELBA C., DAVID K. CALDWELL, and WILLIAM E. EVANS. "Sounds and Behavior of Captive Amazon Freshwater Dolphins, *Inia geoffrensis,*" *Contributions in Science,* no. 108. Los Angeles: Los Angeles County Museum of Natural History, July 25, 1966.

CIAMPI, ELGIN. *Those Other People the Porpoises.* New York: Grosset & Dunlap, 1972.

COOK, JOSEPH J., and WILLIAM L. WISNER. *Warrior Whale.* New York: Dodd, Mead & Company, 1966.

COUSTEAU, JACQUES. Mammals in the Sea, Vol. X: *The Ocean World of Jacques Cousteau.* New York: World Publishing Company, 1973.

———— and PHILIPPE DIOLÉ. *Dolphins.* Trans. J. F. Bernard. New York: Doubleday & Company, 1975.

———— and PHILIPPE DIOLÉ. *Octopus and Squid.* Trans. J. F. Bernard. New York: Doubleday & Company, 1973.

DAWBIN, W. H. "The Seasonal Migratory Cycle of Humpback Whales," in *Whales, Dolphins, and Porpoises,* ed. K. S. Norris. Berkeley and Los Angeles: University of California Press, 1966, pp. 145–70.

EARLE, SYLVIA A. "The Gentle Whales," *National Geographic,* Vol. 155 (1982), no. 1, pp. 2–17.

ELLIS, RICHARD. *The Book of Sharks.* New York: Grosset & Dunlap, 1976.

————. *The Book of Whales.* New York: Alfred A. Knopf, 1982.

————. *Dolphins and Porpoises.* New York: Alfred A. Knopf, 1982.

ENGEL, LEONARD, et al. *The Sea.* New York: Time-Life Books, 1969.

FRASER, F. C. "Comments on the Delphinoidae," in *Whales, Dolphins, and Porpoises,* ed. K. S. Norris. Berkeley and Los Angeles: University of California Press, 1966, pp. 7–31.

GRZIMEK, BERNHARD. *Grzimek's Animal Life Encyclopedia.* New York: Van Nostrand-Reinhold, 1975.

HALL, E. R., and K. R. KELSON. "Order Cetacea—Cetaceans," in *The Mammals of North America,* Vol. II. New York: The Ronald Press Co., 1959, pp. 806–40.

HANDLEY, C. O., JR. "A Synopsis of the Genus *Kogia* (Pygmy Sperm Whales)," in *Whales, Dolphins, and Porpoises,* ed. K. S. Norris. Berkeley and Los Angeles: University of California Press, 1966, pp. 62–69.

HARMER, SIR SIDNEY F. "On Commerson's Dolphin and Other Species of *Cephalorhynchus,*" *Proc. Zool. Soc.* XLIII (1922), 3 pls.

HERALD, E. S. *Living Fishes of the World.* New York: Doubleday & Company, 1961.

HERSHKOVITZ, P. *Catalogue of Living Whales.* United States National Museum. Bulletin 246 (1966).

HILL, D. O., in collaboration with R. ELLIS. "Vanishing Giants," *Audubon,* 1975.

HOY, CHARLES M. "The White-Flag Dolphin of the Tung Ting Lake," *China Jour. of Sci. and Arts,* Vol. 1 (1923), pp. 154–57, 1 pl.

HOYT, E. *The Whale Called Killer.* New York: E. P. Dutton, 1981.

IDYLL, C. P. "Ambergris—Neptune's Treasure," *Smithsonian Report for 1959.* Pub. 4401 (1960) Smithsonian Institution, pp. 377–83, 3 pls.

IRVING, LAWRENCE. "Elective Regulation of the Circulation in Diving Animals," in *Whales, Dolphins, and Porpoises,* ed. K. S. Norris. Berkeley and Los Angeles: University of California Press, 1966, pp. 380–96.

JONES, E. C. "*Isistius brasiliensis,* a squaloid shark, the probable cause of crater wounds on fishes and cetaceans," *U.S. Fisheries Bulletin* 69 (1971), pp. 791–98.

JONSGARD, AGE. "The Distribution of Balaenopteridae in the North Atlantic Ocean," in *Whales, Dolphins, and Porpoises,* ed. K. S. Norris. Berkeley and Los Angeles: University of California Press, 1966, pp. 114–24.

KANWISHER, JOHN, and GUNNAR SUNDNES. "Thermal Regulation in Cetaceans," in *Whales, Dolphins, and Porpoises,* ed. K. S. Norris. Berkeley and Los Angeles: University of California Press, 1966, pp. 397–409.

KELLOGG, R. "Whales, giants of the sea," *National Geographic,* Vol. 77 (1940), no. 1, pp. 35–90, 31 pls.

KELLOGG, W. N. *Porpoises and Sonar.* Chicago: University of Chicago Press, 1961.

LANE, FRANK W. *Kingdom of the Octopus; The Life History of the Cephalopod.* London: Jarrolds, 1957.

LEATHERWOOD, S., W. E. EVANS, and D. W. RICE. "The Whales, Dolphins and Porpoises of the Eastern North Pacific; A Guide to Their Identification in the Water," NUC TP 282. March 1971. D. 83, Technical Information Division, NOAA, Washington, D.C.

LEY, WILLY, et al. *The Poles.* New York: Time-Life Books, 1962.

LINCOLN, ROGER J. "British Marine Amphopoda: Gammaridea." *British Museum of Natural History,* London, 1979.

LINEHAN, EDWARD J. "The Trouble with Dolphins," *National Geographic,* Vol. 155 (1979), no. 4, pp. 506–41.

MACKINTOSH, N. A. "The Distribution of Southern Blue and Fin Whales," in *Whales, Dolphins, and Porpoises,* ed. K. S. Norris. Berkeley and Los Angeles: University of California Press, 1966, pp. 125–44.

MANSFIELD, A. W., T. G. SMITH, and B. BECK. "The Narwhal, *Monodon monoceros,* in Eastern Canadian Waters," *Journal of the Fisheries Research Board of Canada,* Vol. 32 (1975) (7): 1041–46.

MATTHEWS, L. H., ed. *The Whale.* New York: Simon & Schuster, 1968.

McCORMICK, H. W., TOM ALLEN, and W. E. YOUNG. *Shadows in the Sea.* New York: Chilton Books, 1963.

McINTYRE, JOAN. *Mind in the Waters.* New York: Charles Scribner's Sons, 1974.

MEAD, J. G. "Preliminary Report on the Former Net Fisheries for *Tursiops truncatus* in the Western North Atlantic," *Journal of the Fisheries Research Board of Canada,* Vol. 32 (1975) (7): 1155–62.

———, D. K. ODELL, R. S. WELLS, and M. D. SCOTT. "Observations on a mass stranding of spinner dolphin, *Stenella longirostris,* from the west coast of Florida," *U.S. Fisheries Bulletin,* 78 (1980) (2): 353–60.

——— and ROGER S. PAYNE. "A Specimen of the Tasman Beaked Whale, *Tasmacetus Shepherdi,* from Argentina," *Journal of Mammalogy,* Vol. 56 (1975), no. 1, pp. 213–18.

MERCER, M. C. "Modified Leslie-DeLury Population Models of the Long-Finned Pilot Whale *(Globicephala melaena)* and Annual Production of the Short-Finned Squid *(Illex illecebrosus)* Based on Their Interaction at Newfoundland," *Journal of the Fisheries Research Board of Canada,* Vol. 32 (1975) (7): 1145–54.

MITCHELL, E. "Pigmentation pattern evolution in delphinid cetaceans: an essay in adaptive coloration," *Canadian Journal of Zoology,* Vol. 48 (1970), pp. 717–40 + 15 pls.

———. "The Status of the World's Whales," *Nature Canada,* Vol. 2(4) (Dec. 1973), pp. 9–25.

——— and V. M. KOZICKI. "Autumn Stranding of a Northern Bottlenose Whale *(Hyperoodon ampullatus)* in the Bay of Fundy, Nova Scotia," *Journal of the Fisheries Research Board of Canada,* Vol. 32 (1975) (7): 1019–40.

MOORE, J. C. "Diagnosis and Distribution of Beaked Whales of the Genus *Mesoplodon* Known from American Waters," in *Whales, Dolphins, and Porpoises,* ed. K. S. Norris. Berkeley and Los Angeles: University of California Press, 1966, pp. 32–61.

MOWAT, F. *A Whale for the Killing.* Toronto: McClelland and Stewart, 1972.

NICKLIN, FLIP. "New Light on the Singing Whales," *National Geographic,* Vol. 161 (1982), no. 4, pp. 463–77.

NISHIWAKI, MASAHARU. "A Discussion of Rarities Among the Smaller Cetaceans

Caught in Japanese Waters," in *Whales, Dolphins, and Porpoises,* ed. K. S. Norris. Berkeley and Los Angeles: University of California Press, 1966, pp. 192–204.

————. "Distribution and Migration of the Larger Cetaceans in the North Pacific as Shown by Japanese Whaling Results," in *Whales, Dolphins, and Porpoises,* ed. K. S. Norris. Berkeley and Los Angeles: University of California Press, 1966, pp. 171–91.

————. "Ecological Aspects of Smaller Cetaceans, with Emphasis on the Striped Dolphin *(Stenella coeruleoalba),*" *Journal of the Fisheries Research Board of Canada,* Vol. 32 (1975) (7): 1069–72.

NORMAN, J. R., and F. C. FRASER. *Giant Fishes, Whales and Dolphins.* London: Putnam, 1937.

NORRIS, K. S. *The Porpoise Watcher.* New York: W. W. Norton & Company, 1974.

————, ed. *Whales, Dolphins, and Porpoises.* Berkeley and Los Angeles: University of California Press, 1966, rep. 1977.

———— and W. N. MCFARLAND. "A new porpoise of the genus *Phocoena* from the Gulf of California," *Journal of Mammalogy,* 39 (1958): 22–39.

ODELL, D. K. "Status and Aspects of the Life History of the Bottlenose Dolphin, *Tursiops truncatus,* in Florida," *Journal of the Fisheries Research Board of Canada,* Vol. 32 (1975) (7): 1055–58.

OLIVER, W. R. B. "A Pied Variety of the Coastal Porpoise," *Dominion Museum Records in Zoology,* Vol. I (April 1946), pp. 1–4, 3 figs.

————. *"Tasmacetus shepherdi:* A new genus and species of beaked whale from New Zealand," Proc. Zool. Soc. London, ser. B, 107: 371–81.

OMURA, HIDEO. "Bryde's Whale in the Northwest Pacific," in *Whales, Dolphins, and Porpoises,* ed. K. S. Norris. Berkeley and Los Angeles: University of California Press, 1966, pp. 70–78.

PAYNE, ROGER. "Humpbacks: Their Mysterious Songs," *National Geographic,* Vol. 155 (1979), no. 1, pp. 18–25.

PERRIN, W. F. "Distribution and Differentiation of Populations of Dolphins of the Genus *Stenella* in the Eastern Tropical Pacific," *Journal of the Fisheries Research Board of Canada,* Vol. 32 (1975) (7): 1059–67.

————, E. D. MITCHELL, J. G. MEAD, D. K. CALDWELL, and P. J. H. VAN BREE. *"Stenella clymene,* a Rediscovered Tropical Dolphin of the Atlantic," *Journal of Mammalogy,* Vol. 62 (1981), no. 3, pp. 583–98.

PILLERI, GIORGIO. *Die Geheimnisse der blinden Delphine.* Bern and Stuttgart: Hallwag Verlag, 1975.

RIDGEWAY, S. H., ed. *Mammals of the Sea: Biology and Medicine.* Springfield, Ill.: Charles C. Thomas, 1972.

RIES, F. A., and O. R. LANGWORTHY. "A Study of the Surface Structure of the Brain of the Whale *(Balaenoptera Physalus* and *Physeter Catodon),*" *Journal of Comparative Neurology,* Vol. 68 (1937), pp. 1–36, 2 figs., 5 pls.

ROSS, GRAHAM J. B. *Smaller cetaceans of the southeast coast of southern Africa.* Port Elizabeth, South Africa: University of Port Elizabeth, 1979.

————, P. B. BEST, and B. G. DONNELLY. "New Records of the Pygmy Right Whale *(Caperea marginata)* from South Africa, with Comments on Distribution, Migration, Appearance and Behavior," *Journal of the Fisheries Research Board of Canada,* Vol. 32 (1975) (7): 1005–17.

SCAMMON, C. M. *The Marine Mammals of the Northwestern Coast of America, Described and Illustrated: Together with an Account of the American Whale-Fishery.* San Francisco: Carmany and Co., 1874.

SCHEFFER, VICTOR B. *The Year of the Whale.* New York: Charles Scribner's Sons, 1969.

———. *A Natural History of Marine Mammals.* New York: Charles Scribner's Sons, 1976.

SCHEVILL, W. E., ed. *The Whale Problem.* Cambridge, Mass.: Harvard University Press, 1974.

SCORESBY, WILLIAM, JR. *An Account of the Arctic Regions with History and a Description of the Northern Whale-Fishery.* Edinburgh: Archibald Constable, 1820 (1969 edition).

———. *Journal of a Voyage to the Northern Whale-Fishery; Including Researches and Discoveries on the Eastern Coast of West Greenland, Made in the Summer of 1822, in the Ship Baffin of Liverpool.* Edinburgh: Archibald Constable and Co., 1823.

SERGEANT, D. E., and P. F. BRODIE. "Identity, Abundance, and Present Status of Populations of White Whales, *Delphinapterus leucas,* in North America," *Journal of the Fisheries Research Board of Canada,* Vol. 32 (1975) (7): 1047–54.

SLIJPER, E. J. *Whales.* New York: Basic Books, 1962. Trans. A. J. Pomerans.

SMALL, G. *The Blue Whale.* New York: Columbia University Press, 1971.

TARPY, CLIFF. "Killer Whale Attack!" *National Geographic,* Vol. 155 (1979), no. 4, pp. 542–45.

TAVOLGA, MARGARET C. "Behavior of the Bottlenose Dolphin *(Tursiops truncatus);* Social Interactions in a Captive Colony," in *Whales, Dolphins, and Porpoises,* ed. K. S. Norris. Berkeley and Los Angeles: University of California Press, 1966, pp. 718–30.

"The California Gray Whale." *Marine Fisheries Review.* Vol. 36, no. 4 (April 1974): 1–64.

VAN BREE, P. J. H. "On the validity of the subspecies *Cephalorhynchus hectori bicolor* Oliver," *Investigations on Cetacea* 4 (1946): 182–86.

WALKER, ERNEST P., et al. *Mammals of the World.* 3 vols. Baltimore: The Johns Hopkins Press, 1968.

WALKER, T. J. "The California gray whale comes back," *National Geographic,* 139 (1971) (3): 394–415.

WALKER, W. A. "Review of the Live-Capture Fishery for Smaller Cetaceans Taken in Southern California Waters for Public Display, 1966–1973," *Journal of the Fisheries Research Board of Canada,* Vol. 32 (1975) (7): 1197–1211.

ZHOU KAIYA, CH'IAN WEICHUAN, and LI YUEMIN. "Investigations on the Distribution of the Baiji *(Lipotes vexillifer* Miller)." Smithsonian Institution, 1977, copy of a translation of the Chinese article.